LINCOLN'S LAST DAYS

The Shocking Assassination That Changed America Forever

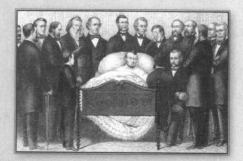

BILL O'REILLY

AND DWIGHT JON ZIMMERMAN

SQUARE
FISH

Henry Holt and Company · NEW YORK

SQUARE
FISH

An Imprint of Macmillan
175 Fifth Avenue
New York, NY 10010
mackids.com

Square Fish and the Square Fish logo are trademarks of Macmillan and
are used by Henry Holt and Company under license from Macmillan.

Square Fish books may be purchased for business or promotional use. For information on bulk
purchases, please contact the Macmillan Corporate and Premium Sales Department at
(800) 221-7945 x5442 or by e-mail at specialmarkets@macmillan.com.

Library of Congress Cataloging-in-Publication Data
O'Reilly, Bill.
Lincoln's last days : the shocking assassination that changed
America forever / Bill O'Reilly and Dwight Jon Zimmerman.
        p.   cm.
Includes bibliographical references and index.
ISBN 978-1-250-04429-7 (paperback) / ISBN 978-0-8050-9676-7 (e-book)
ISBN 978-1-4272-2670-9 (audio)
1. Lincoln, Abraham, 1809–1865—Assassination—Juvenile literature.
I. Zimmerman, Dwight Jon. II. O'Reilly, Bill Killing Lincoln. III. Title.
E457.5.O75 2012 973.7092—dc23   2012016121

Based on the book *Killing Lincoln* by Bill O'Reilly,
published by Henry Holt and Company, LLC.
Lincoln's Last Days originally published in the United States by
Henry Holt and Company, LLC.
First Square Fish Edition: 2014
Book designed by Meredith Pratt / Maps by Gene Thorp
Square Fish logo designed by Filomena Tuosto

1   3   5   7   9   10   8   6   4   2

AR: 7.5 / LEXILE: 1020L

LINCOLN'S LAST DAYS

nor long remember, what we say here, but
can never forget what they did here. It is
for us, the living, rather to be dedicated
here to the unfinished work which they have,
thus far, so nobly carried on. It is rather
for us to be here dedicated to the great
task remaining before us— that from these
honored dead we take increased devotion
to that cause for which they here gave
the last full measure of devotion— that
we here highly resolve that these dead
shall not have died in vain; that this
nation shall have a new birth of freedom;
and that this government of the people, by
the people, for the people, shall not perish
from the earth.

BY BILL O'REILLY

Lincoln's Last Days
Kennedy's Last Days
The Last Days of Jesus

For Makeda Wubneh,
who makes the world a better place
—B. O'R.

For Eleanor and Albert Law
—D. J. Z.

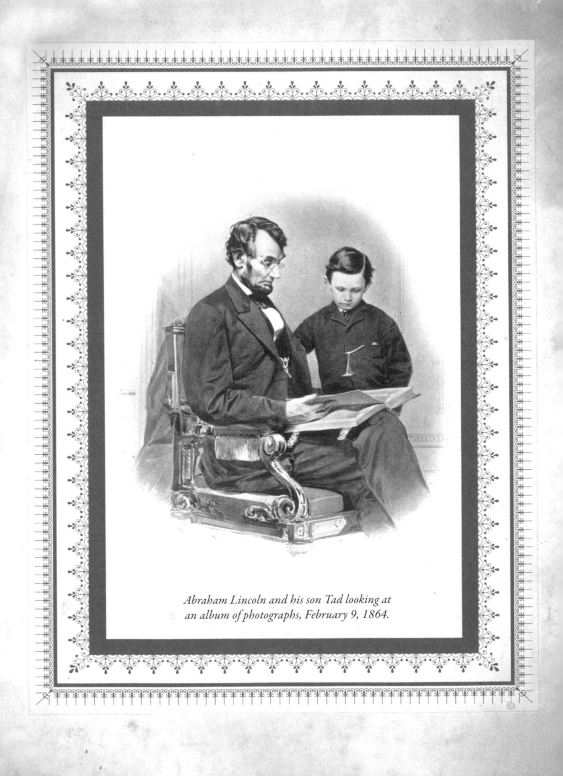

Abraham Lincoln and his son Tad looking at an album of photographs, February 9, 1864.

CONTENTS

A Note to Readers

YOU ARE ABOUT TO READ a true story that took place more than 140 years ago—the story of one of America's saddest events. Just days after the end of the American Civil War, President Abraham Lincoln was assassinated. President Lincoln had led this country through the bloodiest war in its history. He had reason to hope that the nation would be united again.

Abraham Lincoln was betrayed by his countrymen. He died within months of his fifty-sixth birthday and before he could complete his life's work. The tragedy that befell Lincoln should be known by every American. His life and death continue to shape us as a people, even today. America is a great country, but like every other nation on earth, it is influenced by evil. John Wilkes Booth epitomizes the evil that can harm us, even as President Abraham Lincoln represents the good that can make us stronger. I think that Abraham Lincoln is one of our strongest, bravest, and most

Abraham Lincoln delivers his Gettysburg Address
at the Gettysburg National Cemetery, November 19, 1863.

exemplary leaders. As you read about his last days, I hope you will come to understand what made him great.

Before I began researching this book, I *thought* I understood the story of President Lincoln's assassination. But even though I used to teach history in a high school, there were aspects of the events that were new to me and that will be new to you. This is a story of courage, cowardice, and betrayal. President Lincoln's great courage was met with the bitter anger and hatred of people who could not accept that the Union army had won the war. As you read about this time in our country's history, think about what we can learn from this event.

I love American history. I collect letters signed by presidents and photographs and drawings depicting presidents and important events. One of my favorites is a signed photograph of Abraham Lincoln. Looking at that photograph of President Lincoln, I wonder what he was thinking. In this book I have used his words and many other primary sources to bring his last days to life. Here is the story of the best kind of American. I am proud to share it with you.

[signature]

New York
May 2012

Key Players

President Abraham Lincoln, Family, Cabinet, Staff, and Others

William Crook: Lincoln's bodyguard.

James Ford: Manager of Ford's Theatre.

Clara Harris: Major Henry Reed Rathbone's fiancée.

Andrew Johnson: Vice president during Lincoln's second term.

Laura Keene: British-born American theater actress.

Ward Hill Lamon: Former Lincoln law partner, Lincoln's self-appointed bodyguard.

Dr. Charles Augustus Leale: The first doctor to reach the president after he had been shot.

Abraham Lincoln: Sixteenth president of the United States.

Mary Todd Lincoln: Abraham Lincoln's wife.

Robert Lincoln: Lincoln's eldest child.

John Parker: Assigned to guard the president on the night of the assassination.

Major Henry Reed Rathbone: A guest of the Lincolns at Ford's Theatre.

William Henry Seward: Secretary of state.

Edwin McMaster Stanton: Secretary of war.

Lincoln Assassination Conspirators, Friends, Associates, and Captors

George Atzerodt: Conspirator.

Lafayette Curry Baker: Spy, detective, and leader of the group that finds John Wilkes Booth.

John Wilkes Booth: Famous actor and President Lincoln's assassin.

Sergeant Boston Corbett: The Union soldier who shoots Booth.

Samuel Cox: Farmer who provides temporary refuge for Booth and Herold.

Richard Garrett: The farmer in whose barn Booth and Herold are captured.

William Garrett: One of Richard Garrett's two sons who guard the barn where Booth and Herold hide.

John Wilkes Booth.

David Herold: Conspirator.

Thomas Jones: Smuggler who helps Booth and Herold cross the Potomac River.

Dr. Samuel Mudd: Provide Booth and Herold temporary refuge.

Lewis Powell (aka Lewis Payne): Conspirator.

Edmund "Ned" Spangler: Stagehand at Ford's Theatre.

Anna Surratt: Mary Surratt's daughter.

John Surratt, Jr.: Mary Surratt's son and the only Lincoln assassination conspirator not to be tried and convicted.

Mary Surratt: The owner of a boardinghouse known to be used by Confederate sympathizers.

Union Army Officers and Soldiers

Brigadier General of Volunteers George Armstrong Custer: Cavalry division commander under Major General Philip Sheridan.

Lieutenant Johnston Livingston de Peyster: Chief of staff of the Army of the Potomac's Twenty-fifth Corps.

Lieutenant General Ulysses S. Grant: General in chief of all the Union armies in 1865.

Major General George Gordon Meade: Commanding general of the Army of the Potomac.

Major General Philip "Little Phil" Sheridan: Commander of the Army of the Potomac's Cavalry Corps.

Colonel Francis Washburn: Commanding officer of the Fourth Massachusetts Cavalry.

Major General Horatio Wright: Commanding officer of the Army of the Potomac's Sixth Corps.

The flag of the Union army.

Confederate States of America

Major General Richard "Fighting Dick" Anderson: Commanding general of the Army of Northern Virginia's Fourth Corps.

Jefferson Davis: First and only president of the Confederate States of America.

Major General John B. Gordon: Division commander in the Army of Northern Virginia.

Lieutenant General A. P. Hill: Commanding officer of the Army of Northern Virginia's Third Corps.

General Joseph E. Johnston: Commander of the Army of Tennessee.

General Robert E. Lee: Commanding general of the Army of Northern Virginia and general in chief of all the Confederate armies in 1865.

Lieutenant General James "Pete" Longstreet: Commanding officer of the Army of Northern Virginia's First Corps.

Major General Thomas Lafayette Rosser: Cavalry division commander in the Army of Northern Virginia.

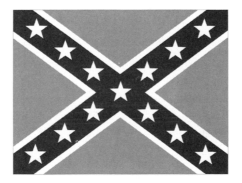

A battle flag of the Confederate States of America.

SATURDAY, MARCH 4, 1865
Washington, D.C.

ABRAHAM LINCOLN, the man with six weeks to live, is anxious. The speech he is about to give is vital to the peace of the country. Since the Battle of Fort Sumter took place in South Carolina in April 1861, the United States has been a "house divided," locked in a civil war between the free North and the slaveholding South. Led by South Carolina, a total of eleven slaveholding states in the South have left the Union and formed a separate nation, the Confederate States of America. The states that seceded felt that maintaining the institution of slavery was essential to their economy and they were willing to leave the Union rather than outlaw slavery.

Lincoln tried to stop the states from leaving, but they refused his peaceful appeals. When Confederate troops fired on Union troops at Fort Sumter, Lincoln had no choice but to go to war. This civil war has not only divided the nation, it has also split countless families, pitting fathers against sons, and brothers against brothers. It is

Abraham Lincoln delivering his second inaugural address, March 4, 1865.
John Wilkes Booth is in the crowd to the right and above where the president stands.

a situation that even affects Lincoln's family. His wife, Mary Todd Lincoln, has relatives fighting for the Confederacy. Much blood—too much blood—has been shed in this terrible conflict. Lincoln sighs, hoping that it will end soon, and with the Union victorious.

Fifty thousand men and women are standing in pouring rain and ankle-deep mud to watch Abraham Lincoln take the oath of office to begin his second term.

Lincoln steps up to the podium and delivers an eloquent appeal for reunification in his second inaugural address.

"With malice toward none, with charity for all, with firmness in the right as God gives us to see the right, let us strive on to finish the work we are in, to bind up the nation's wounds, to care for him who shall have borne the battle and for his widow and his orphan, to do all which may achieve and cherish a just and lasting peace among ourselves and with all nations," the president says humbly. As he speaks, the sun bursts through the clouds, its light surrounding the tall and outwardly serene Lincoln.

Although Lincoln does not know this, 120 miles south of Washington, at the important railroad and communications center of Petersburg, Virginia, a siege that started in June 1864 is nearing its end. The Confederate Army of Northern Virginia, under the command of General Robert E. Lee, has been pinned in and around the city for more than 250 days by Union forces under the command of General Ulysses S. Grant. Lee knew if he didn't defend Petersburg, the road to the Confederate capital of Richmond would be wide open. The capture of Richmond by Union troops would be a powerful symbolic victory, telling everyone that the end of the Confederacy was near. So Lee ordered his army to stay, dig trenches, and fight.

But now, in April 1865, Lee's army is weak. At this point, if Lee remains and continues to defend Petersburg, his forces will be destroyed by Grant's Army of the Potomac, which grows stronger in men and guns with each passing week. Lee knows that Grant is preparing for an overwhelming attack. Lee plans to have his army slip out of Petersburg and escape south to the Carolinas before that happens. If he succeeds, Lincoln's prayer for a reunified United States of America may never be answered. America will continue to be divided into a North and a South, a United States of America and a Confederate States of America.

◆◆━━◆◆◆◆◆━━◆◆

Lincoln's inaugural speech is a performance worthy of a great dramatic actor. And indeed, one of America's most famous actors stands just yards away as the president speaks. Twenty-six-year-old John Wilkes Booth is inspired by the president's words—though not in the way Lincoln intends.

The president has ambitious plans for his second term in office. Ending the war and healing the war-torn nation are Lincoln's overriding ambitions. He will use every last bit of his trademark determination to see these goals realized; nothing must stand in his way.

But evil knows no boundaries. And a most powerful evil—in the person of John Wilkes Booth and his fellow conspirators—is now focused on Abraham Lincoln.

John Wilkes Booth.

PART ONE

THE BEGINNING OF THE END OF THE WAR

Lieutenant General Ulysses S. Grant,
United States Army.

General Robert E. Lee,
Confederate States of America.

Chapter 1

SUNDAY, APRIL 2, 1865
Petersburg, Virginia

THERE IS NO NORTH VERSUS SOUTH in Petersburg now. Only Grant versus Lee—and Grant has the upper hand. Like many of the generals on both sides, Lee and Grant served together in the Mexican War. Now, in the Civil War, these former comrades-in-arms are enemies.

Lee is fifty-eight years old, a tall, rugged Virginian with a silver beard and formal air. Grant is forty-two and Lee's exact opposite: dark-haired and sloppy in dress, a small, introspective man who has a fondness for cigars and a close relationship with horses. When Grant was a baby, his mother's friends were shocked to see that Hannah Grant allowed her son to crawl between their horses' feet!

Like Lee, Grant possesses a genius for warfare—indeed, he is capable of little else. When the Civil War began, he was a washed-up, barely employed West Point graduate and veteran of the Mexican War who had been forced out of military service, done in by lonely western outposts and an inability to hold his liquor. It was only

through luck and connections that Grant secured a commission in an Illinois regiment. At the battles of Fort Henry and Fort Donelson in Tennessee in February 1862, Grant and his army delivered the first major victories to the Union. And Grant kept on winning. As the war continued, Lincoln gave him more and more responsibility. Now Grant is general in chief—the commander of all the Union armies from Virginia down to New Orleans.

At Petersburg, the Confederate lines are arranged in a jagged horseshoe, facing south— thirty-seven miles of trenches and fortifications in all. The outer edges of the horseshoe are two miles from the city center, under the commands of Confederate A. P. Hill on the right and John B. Gordon on the left.

The day before, at the decisive Battle of Five Forks, Union General Phil Sheridan and 45,000 men had captured a pivotal crossing, cutting off the main road to North Carolina.

It was long after dark when word of the great victory reached Grant. Without pausing, Grant pushed his advantage. He ordered another attack. He hoped this would be the blow to crush Lee and his army once and for all. His soldiers would attack just before dawn, but he ordered the artillery fire to begin immediately.

A Currier & Ives lithograph of the Battle of Petersburg.

The Union attack is divided into two waves. Major General Horatio Wright, leading the 24,000 men in his Sixth Corps, charges first and shatters the right side of Lee's line. Wright's attack is so well choreographed that many of his soldiers are literally miles in front of the main Union force. As Wright's men reorganize to

Lieutenant General A. P. Hill,
Confederate States of America.

prepare for the next stage of attack, the rest of the Union army strikes.

Meanwhile, Lee and his assistants, the generals James "Pete" Longstreet and A. P. Hill, gaze out at Wright's army from the front porch of Lee's Confederate headquarters, the Turnbull house. The three of them stand there as the sun rises high enough to confirm their worst fears: every soldier they can see wears blue.

A horrified A. P. Hill realizes that his army is being crushed, and he jumps on his horse to try to stop the disaster in the making. He is shot and killed by Union soldiers.

Lee faces the sobering fact that Union soldiers are just a few short steps from controlling the main road he plans to use for his retreat. He will be cut off if the bluecoats in the pasture continue their advance.

Fortune, however, is smiling on the Confederates. Those Union soldiers have no idea that Lee himself is right in front of them. If they did, they would attack without ceasing, because any soldier who captured Lee would become a legend.

The Union scouts can clearly see the small artillery battery outside Lee's headquarters, and they assume that it is part of a much larger rebel force hiding out of sight. Rather than rush forward, the scouts hesitate.

Seizing the moment, Lee escapes north across the Appomattox River and then turns west. His goal is the Richmond and Danville Railroad Line at Amelia Court House, where he has arranged to store food and supplies. He issues orders to the commanders of his corps to follow. At one point, Lee pauses to write a letter to Confederate president Jefferson Davis, saying that his army is in retreat and can no longer defend Richmond. Davis and the Confederate government must abandon the city or risk capture.

The final chase has begun.

Lieutenant General
James "Pete" Longstreet.

Chapter 2

MONDAY, APRIL 3, 1865
Petersburg, Virginia

LEE'S RETREAT IS UNRULY AND TIME-CONSUMING, despite the sense of urgency. Grant watches the bridges—they are packed with Confederate soldiers. A cannon barrage could kill hundreds instantly, and Grant's cannons are certainly close enough to do the job. All he has to do is give the command.

But he hesitates.

For now, his plan is to capture the Confederates, not to kill them. Grant has already taken many prisoners. He watches these rebels escape, scheming to find a way to capture even more.

Grant hands a courier the orders. Then he telegraphs President Lincoln. Earlier in the week, he had sent the president a message, asking him to come to City Point to witness the capture of Petersburg. Now, with Lee's army out of Petersburg and the Union army in control of the city, Grant asks the president to meet him there.

As soon as the Army of Northern Virginia began retreating from Petersburg, Grant had ordered part of his army to head north and capture Richmond. Now he hopes to hear about the battle for Richmond before the president arrives. Capturing Lee's army is of the utmost importance, but both Grant and Lincoln also believe that a Confederacy without a capital is a doomsday scenario for the rebels. Delivering the news that Richmond has fallen would be a delightful way to kick off their meeting.

The sound of horseshoes on cobblestones echoes down the quiet street. It's Lincoln. Stepping down from his horse, Lincoln walks through the main gate of the house Grant has chosen for their meeting. He takes the walkway in long, eager strides, a smile suddenly stretching across his face,

General Grant on the front cover of the July 25, 1863, issue of Harper's Weekly, *an illustrated news magazine.*

his deep fatigue vanishing at the sight of his favorite general. When he shakes Grant's hand, it is with great gusto.

The two men sit on the veranda, taking no notice of the cold. Their conversation shows deep mutual respect. Lincoln and Grant talk for ninety minutes. Although Grant had hoped to receive word of Richmond's fall while he was with the president, too much time has passed. He must leave to join his army and continue the pursuit of Lee. President Lincoln and General Grant shake hands, then Grant gallops off to join the Army of the Potomac.

Before leaving, Lincoln also shakes hands with some people in the crowd gathered in front of the meeting place. He then rides back to City Point. The way is littered with hundreds of dead soldiers, their unburied bodies swollen by death and sometimes stripped bare by scavengers. Lincoln doesn't look away.

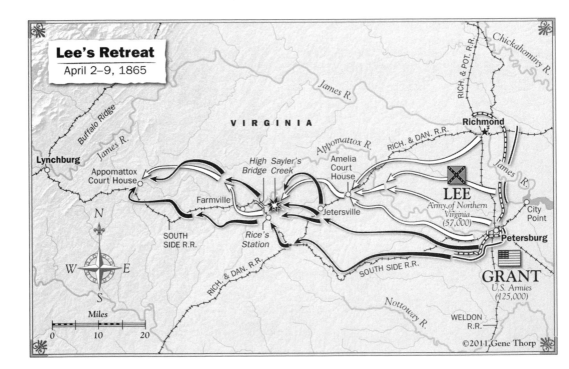

Upon his return to City Point, he receives the reward Grant had hoped to deliver personally. A courier hands the president a telegram informing him that Richmond has fallen.

"Thank God that I have lived to see this," Lincoln cries. "It seems to me that I have been dreaming a horrid dream for four years, and now the nightmare is gone."

But the nightmare's not really gone. President Lincoln has just twelve days to live.

Chapter 3

TUESDAY, APRIL 4, 1865
Richmond, Virginia

Abraham Lincoln stands on the deck of the USS *Malvern* as the warship chugs slowly and cautiously up the James River toward Richmond. The channel is choked with burning warships and the floating corpses of horses. Deadly antiship mines known as torpedoes bob on the surface, drifting with the current, ready to explode the instant they come into contact with a vessel.

The Confederate capital is now in Union hands. Lincoln can clearly see that Richmond—or what's left of it—barely resembles the refined city it was. The sunken ships and torpedoes in the harbor tell only some of the story. Part of Richmond is gone, burned to the ground.

A lithograph showing the burning of Richmond, Virginia, and its evacuation.

When it becomes too dangerous for the *Malvern* to get any closer, Lincoln is rowed to shore. Finally, he steps from the barge and up onto a landing.

What Lincoln sees now can only be described as shocking.

The Confederate attempt to destroy supplies and arms to keep them out of the approaching Union army's hands has escalated out of control. In a cruel irony, it was not the Union army that laid waste to the city. Richmond was destroyed by its own sons.

Richmond had still been in flames on the morning of April 3, when the Union troops arrived. Brick facades and chimneys still

The USS Malvern. *Note the paddle wheel and smokestack in the middle of the ship, as well as the masts for sails at both the bow and stern. This ship could use either wind or steam power.*

stood, but wooden frames and roofs had been incinerated. Smoldering ruins and the sporadic whistle of artillery greeted the Twenty-fourth and Twenty-fifth Corps of the Union army.

The instant the long blue line marched into town, the slaves of Richmond were free. They were stunned to see that the Twenty-fifth contained black soldiers from a new branch of the army known as the USCT—the United States Colored Troops.

Lieutenant Johnston Livingston de Peyster, a member of the staff of Twenty-fifth Corps commander Major General Godfrey Wetzel, galloped his horse straight to the capitol building. "I sprang from my horse," he wrote proudly, and "rushed up to the roof." In his hand was an American flag. Dashing to the flagpole, he hoisted the Stars and Stripes over Richmond. The city was Confederate no more.

That particular flag had thirty-six stars, a new number, because of Nevada's recent admission to the Union. By tradition, this new flag would not become official until the Fourth of July. It was the flag of the America to come—the postwar America, united and expanding. It was, in other words, the flag of Abraham Lincoln's dreams.

Chapter 4

TUESDAY, APRIL 4, 1865
Richmond, Virginia

ABRAHAM LINCOLN HAS NEVER FOUGHT in battle. In his short three-month enlistment during the Black Hawk War in 1832, he never saw combat. He is a politician, and politicians are seldom given the chance to play the role of conquering hero. But this is Lincoln's war. It always has been. To Lincoln goes the honor of conquering hero.

No one knows this better than the freed slaves of Richmond. They gather around Lincoln, so alarming the men who rowed him ashore that they form a protective ring around the president. The sailors maintain this ring around Lincoln as he marches through the city, even as the admiring crowd grows to hundreds.

The white citizens of Richmond, tight-lipped and hollow-eyed, take it all in. They make no move, no gesture, no sound to welcome him. "Every window was crowded with heads," one sailor will

The ruins of Richmond. Note what appears to be smoke still rising from ruins in the center of the photograph.

*The Confederate White House in Richmond, Virginia,
home of President Jefferson Davis.*

remember. "But it was a silent crowd. There was something oppressive in those thousands of watchers without a sound, either of welcome or hatred. I think we would have welcomed a yell of defiance."

Soon Lincoln finds himself on the corner of Twelfth and Clay Streets, staring at the former home of Jefferson Davis. Lincoln steps past the sentry boxes, grasps the wrought-iron railing, and marches up the steps into the Confederate White House.

He is shown into a small room with floor-to-ceiling windows and crossed cavalry swords over the door. "This was President Davis's office," a housekeeper says respectfully.

Lincoln's eyes roam over the elegant wood desk, which Davis

had so thoughtfully tidied before running off two days earlier. "Then this must be President Davis's chair," he says with a grin, sinking into its burgundy padding. He crosses his legs and leans back.

Lincoln can afford to relax. He has Richmond. The Confederacy is doomed. All the president needs now is for Grant to finish the rest of the job, and then he can get to the work of reunification that will be known to history as Reconstruction.

The fireplace and mantel in Confederate president Jefferson Davis's office. Draped above the mantel are the first two flags of the Confederacy: the Stars and Bars (left), and the Stainless Banner (right). Above the crossed flags is a portrait of Jefferson Davis.

Chapter 5

TUESDAY, APRIL 4, 1865
Amelia Court House, Virginia

T HE DAY-AND-A-HALF TRUDGE to Amelia Court House, where Lee and his soldiers hope to find rations, began optimistically enough, with Lee's men happy to finally be away from Petersburg and looking forward to their first real meal in months. Lee's optimism slowly filtered down into the ranks. Against all odds, his men regained their confidence as the trenches of Petersburg receded into the distance.

By the time they reach Amelia Court House, on April 4, electricity sizzles through the ranks. The men are speaking of hope and are confident of victory as they wonder where and when they will fight the Yankees once again.

It's just before noon when they arrive. Lee quietly gives the order to unload the supply train and distribute the food in an organized fashion. The last thing he wants is for his army to give in to their hunger and rush the train. Orderliness is crucial for an effective fighting force.

The train doors are yanked open. Inside, huge wooden containers are stacked floor to ceiling. Lee's excited men hurriedly jerk the boxes down onto the ground and pry them open.

Then, horror!

This is what those boxes contain: 200 crates of ammunition, 164 cartons of artillery harnesses, and 96 carts to carry ammunition.

There is no food.

Lee's optimism is replaced by defeat. "His face was still calm, as it always was," wrote one enlisted man. "But his carriage was no

A Civil War–era railroad train with boxcars. The men are probably guards.

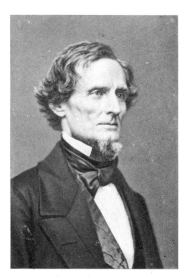

*Jefferson Davis, president of the
Confederate States of America.*

longer erect, as his soldiers had been used to seeing it. The troubles of these last days had already plowed great furrows in his forehead. His eyes were red as if with weeping, his cheeks sunken and haggard, his face colorless. No one who looked upon him then, as he stood there in full view of the disastrous end, can ever forget the intense agony written on his features."

Lee sends wagons out to scour the countryside in search of food. He anxiously awaits their return, praying they will be overflowing with grains and smoked meats and leading calves and pigs to be slaughtered.

The wagons come back empty. The countryside is bare.

Lee must move before Grant finds him. His fallback plan is yet another forced march, this one to the city of Danville, where more than a million rations are supposed to await. Danville, however, is a hundred miles south. As impossible as it is to think of marching an army that far on empty stomachs, it is Lee's only hope.

Chapter 6

WEDNESDAY, APRIL 5, 1865
Amelia Court House, Virginia

A COLD RAIN FALLS ON THE MORNING of April 5. Lee gives the order to move out. It is, in the mind of one Confederate soldier, "the cruelest marching order the commanders had ever given the men in four years of fighting." Units of infantry, cavalry, and artillery begin trudging down the road. Danville is a four-day march—if they have the energy to make it. "It is now," one soldier writes in his diary, "a race of life or death."

They get only seven miles before coming to a dead halt at a Union roadblock outside Jetersville. At first there appears to be no more than a small cavalry force. But a quick look through Lee's field glasses reveals the truth. Union soldiers are digging trenches and fortifications along the road and reinforcing them with fallen trees and fence rails to protect themselves from rebel bullets.

Lee gallops his horse, Traveller, to the front and considers the situation. Sometimes knowing when *not* to fight is just as important to a general's success as knowing *how* to fight.

And this is not a time to fight.

Lee quickly turns his army west in a big loop toward the town of Paineville. The men don't travel down one single road but spread out along a series of parallel roads connecting the hamlets and burgs of rural Virginia. The countryside is rolling and open in some places, forested in others, and sometimes swampy. Creeks and rivers overflow their banks from the recent rains, drenching the troops at every crossing.

Lee marches his men all day, and then all night. At a time when every fiber of their being cries out for sleep and food, they press forward over muddy, rutted roads, enduring rain and chill and the constant harassment of Union cavalry.

On the rare occasions when the army stops to rest, men simply crumple to the ground and sleep. When it is time to march again, officers move from man to man, shaking them awake and ordering them to their feet. Some men refuse to rise and are left sleeping, soon to become Union prisoners. Others can't rise because they're simply too weak. These men, too, are left behind. In this way, Lee's army dwindles. The 30,000 who retreated from Petersburg just three days ago have been reduced by half.

Shortly after midnight, a courier approaches the marching soldiers and hands Lee a captured Union message from Grant to his generals, giving orders to attack at first light.

But at last Lee gets good news in the form of a report from his commissary general, I. M. St. John: 80,000 rations have been rushed

A painting by H. A. Ogden of General Robert E. Lee riding his horse, Traveller.

to the town of Farmville, just nineteen miles away. Lee can be there in a day. He swings his army toward Farmville. It is his final chance to keep the Confederate struggle alive.

An 1865 photograph of High Bridge that spans the Appomattox River near Farmville, Virginia.

Chapter 7

WEDNESDAY, APRIL 5, 1865
Jetersville, Virginia
Night

GENERAL GRANT IS ALSO ON A MIDNIGHT RIDE. The great hooves of his horse beat a tattoo on the bad roads and forest trails of central Virginia. Speed is of the essence. Scouts report that Lee is escaping, marching his men through the night in a bold attempt to reach rations at Farmville. From there, it's just a short march to High Bridge, a stone-and-wood structure wide enough to handle an army. The bridge spans the Appomattox River, separating central and western Virginia. Once Lee crosses and burns the bridge behind him, his escape into North Carolina and the heart of Confederate territory will be complete, and the dreadful war will continue.

Tonight decides everything. Grant is so close to stopping Lee. Grant knows that he must ride hard. Lee must be captured now.

As always, Grant's battle plan is simple: Get in front of Lee. Block his path. Rather than wait until morning, he orders his staff to mount up for the sixteen-mile midnight ride to Jetersville, where

General Sheridan and his cavalry are camped. After speaking with "Little Phil" Sheridan, who enthusiastically agrees to Grant's plan, the two continue on to the headquarters of Major General George G. Meade, the commander of the Army of the Potomac.

◆━◈×◈━◆

When Grant became general in chief of the Union armies, he could have made his headquarters in Washington, D.C. Many people expected him to do that. But Grant hates Washington and its politicians. Instead, he established his headquarters in the field, with the Army of the Potomac. Because of this, people think that Grant

Major General George Gordon Meade, commanding general of the Army of the Potomac.

commands the Army of the Potomac. That is not true—Meade is the commander. But Grant is Meade's boss. So Meade will do what Grant says.

———◆◈◆———

Grant delivers his orders. Sheridan will attack from Lee's front, and Meade from Lee's rear. At first light, Meade's infantry will chase and find Lee's army, then harass them and slow their forward movement. Sheridan, meanwhile, will "put himself south of the enemy and follow him to his death." In this way, the Confederate race to North Carolina will stop dead in its tracks.

Promptly at six A.M., the two armies begin to march.

The Black Thursday of the Confederacy has arrived.

Chapter 8

THURSDAY, APRIL 6, 1865
Rice's Station, Virginia
Dawn

IT HAS NOW BEEN FOUR DAYS since the Confederate army began retreating from Petersburg. For four days, the Army of Northern Virginia has eluded the army of General Grant. Better yet, there are rations waiting just a few miles away, in Farmville.

The plan is for Lee's men to fill their empty bellies in Farmville, then march over High Bridge. Lee will order the bridge burned immediately after they cross, preventing the Union army from following. In a few days, they'll reach North Carolina.

But grim news awaits them when they ride into Rice's Station. A group of Union cavalry galloped through an hour ago. They are now ahead of the Confederates. General Longstreet's scouts report that 800 bluecoats on foot and on horseback are headed for High Bridge. Their goal, obviously, is to burn the bridge and close Lee's escape route.

Lee hears the thunder of approaching hooves. General Thomas

Lafayette Rosser, an outgoing twenty-eight-year-old Texan, gallops his cavalry into Rice's Station.

Longstreet approaches Rosser and, warning him about the Union plan, screams, "Go after the bridge burners. Capture or destroy the detachment, even if it takes the last man of your command to do it."

Rosser salutes. Then he grins and barks the order to his men. The quiet morning air explodes with noise as hundreds of hooves pound into the narrow dirt road.

After they depart, there is nothing Longstreet can do but wait.

An 1865 photograph showing the railroad track and wooden pedestrian walkways on High Bridge.

Chapter 9

THURSDAY, APRIL 6, 1865
Farmville, Virginia
Midmorning

THE UNION FORCE RACING TO BURN High Bridge consists of the Fourth Massachusetts Cavalry, the Fifty-fourth Pennsylvania Infantry, and the 123rd Ohio Infantry.

Colonel Francis Washburn of the Fourth Massachusetts orders his cavalry to gallop ahead of the foot soldiers. His men will burn the bridge while the infantry covers the rear.

As Colonel Washburn and his men arrive within three miles of High Bridge, they are joined by Union general Theodore Read, who has undertaken a daring mission to warn Washburn that the Confederates are hot on his trail and that a small force of rebels who have been at High Bridge for months are dug in around it. Read has full authority to cancel Washburn's mission if he thinks it too risky.

Washburn and Read hold a council of war at a hilltop plantation known as Chatham, roughly halfway between Rice's Station and High Bridge. They can see the bridge in the distance, and the two

An 1865 photograph of High Bridge showing repairs in progress
following the Battle of High Bridge.

dirt forts defending it. General Read orders Washburn to proceed to the bridge. Read will stay behind with the infantry to cover the cavalry's rear. This is a gamble, and both of these brave officers know it.

If it succeeds, they could end the war by sundown.

Washburn's cavalry ride for an hour. But then they are ambushed by rebel cavalry. Washburn, fearing nothing, gives chase. But it's a clever trap. The rebels draw the bluecoats in as they link up with the other Confederate force defending the bridge. Suddenly, Confederate artillery rains down on Washburn and his men.

Washburn is within a quarter mile of the bridge, his force largely intact. But then comes the crackle of gunfire from behind him. Three years of combat experience tells Washburn that he is in trouble; Confederate cavalrymen have found his infantry. High Bridge must wait.

About 1,200 Confederate horsemen wait to attack Washburn's cavalry and infantry, which together number slightly more than 800—but only about 80 of those are cavalry. Rebel horses and riders hold in a long line, awaiting the order to charge and crush the tiny Union force.

Colonel Washburn remains cool, surveying what could be a hopeless situation. Infantry is no match for the speed and agility of cavalry. His infantry lie on their bellies and peer across at Confederate cavalry. They have had no time to dig trenches or build fortifications, so hugging the ground is their only defense. Washburn is cut off from the rest of Grant's army, with no hope of rescue.

He decides that his only hope is to be bold—a quality this Harvard man possesses in abundance.

After conferring with General Read, Washburn orders his tiny cavalry to assemble just out of rifle range, in columns of four, then addresses the ranks. He barks out his plan and reminds the infantry to follow right behind the Union riders to punch a hole through the rebel lines.

On Washburn's command, the Fourth Massachusetts trot their mounts forward. Outnumbered by more than fifteen to one, they shut out all thoughts of this being the last battle of their lives. They ride hard. Their fate comes down to one simple word: "Charge!"

An illustration showing the kind of desperate hand-to-hand fighting that often took place between Union and Confederate cavalry.

The audacity of the Union cavalry charge and its succeed-at-all-costs desperation ignites panic in the rebel force. The battlefield splits in two as Washburn's men punch through the first wave of the rebel line. The Union charge at Chatham, for a brief instant, is a triumph.

But, stunningly, after the cavalry charges, Washburn's infantry does not move. Even as the Confederate defenses crumble, as Washburn organizes his men for the secondary attack that will smash an escape route through the rebel lines, the foot soldiers are still on their bellies, sealing their own doom.

General Rosser senses what's happening and doesn't waste a second. The Texan yells for his Confederate cavalry to counterattack.

The fight becomes a brutal test of courage and horsemanship. "I have been many a day in hot fights," Rosser will marvel later, "but I never saw anything approaching that at High Bridge."

Suddenly, the battle is over.

Major General Philip H. Sheridan.

The Confederates have lost a hundred men.

The Union has lost everyone.

The failure of the Union infantry to obey Washburn's orders to attack determined their fate.

Rosser leads his weary men back toward Rice's Station, content in the knowledge that he has single-handedly saved the Confederacy—for the moment.

Lee will now have his escape. Or at least it appears that way.

Chapter 10

THURSDAY, APRIL 6, 1865
On the Road to Farmville, Virginia
Afternoon

UNION GENERAL GEORGE MEADE'S INFANTRY finally finds the tail end of the Confederate column about ten miles away from the High Bridge fight. A hard rain is falling. In the first of what will be many firefights on this day, small bands of Union soldiers begin shooting at the Confederate rear guard.

Meanwhile, in Rice's Station, Lee assesses the situation. Hearing the ferocity of the firing from High Bridge, he assumes that the Union force is much bigger than the group of men who galloped past him earlier. If Lee had any cavalry at his disposal, they would act as his eyes and ears, scouting ahead and returning with the truth. But he doesn't. Lee can only guess at what's happening—and he guesses wrong.

Fearing that General Sheridan and his Union cavalry have already leapfrogged out in front, Lee holds his men in Rice's Station. At a time when it is crucial to be on the move, he chooses to remain in place.

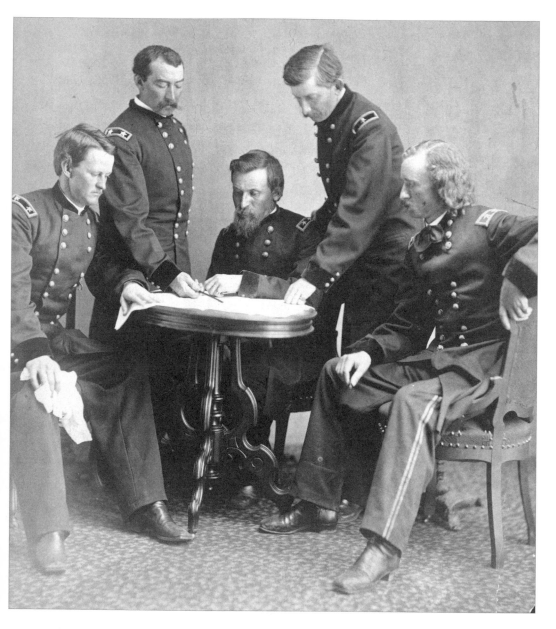

*An 1865 photograph of Major General Philip "Little Phil" Sheridan
meeting with generals under his command. From left to right: Wesley Merritt,
Sheridan, George Crook, James William Forsyth, and George Armstrong Custer.*

As Lee waits, Sheridan's three cavalry divisions are searching high and low for the Army of Northern Virginia. His three commanders are Generals George Armstrong Custer, Thomas Devin, and George Crook. Custer is the youngest and most aggressive, a blond-haired dynamo—he had roomed with the Confederate Thomas Rosser at West Point.

Custer leads the Union cavalry on their search-and-destroy mission against the Confederate column. At midmorning, he discovers the heart of the column, perhaps six miles from High Bridge. Custer does not hesitate. His division attacks. Then, upon meeting resistance, the young general stalls, in order to allow another cavalry division to attack. In this way, he slowly works his way up the Confederate line.

Custer's strategy succeeds. By two P.M. his division pours into the small town of Marshall's Crossroads, where they are met by a lone artillery battalion. The Confederate cannons are no match for Custer's horsemen. He captures the small force and sets the rebel guns ablaze. But then another Confederate force counterattacks, pushing Custer out of the town. The Confederates dig in immediately, knowing that more fighting is imminent. The rebels hope to hold on long enough for Lee's main army to reinforce them.

George Custer, however, is not to be denied. He scribbles a message to Crook and Devin, requesting help. Within an hour, their divisions are on the scene.

All afternoon, the three Union divisions initiate mounted and dismounted cavalry charges against the dug-in rebels.

The rebels, brilliantly led by Major General Richard "Fighting Dick" Anderson, hold fast, repelling each and every charge.

As daylight turns to evening, Custer assembles his men for one final charge. He orders the regimental band to play, hoping to strike fear into the enemy. Seeing the cavalry, Confederate officers call an immediate retreat. Their goal is to reach Lee at Rice's Station.

Custer and the Union cavalry ride fast and hard into Anderson's lines before they can escape. More than 2,600 Confederates are captured.

Brigadier General
Thomas C. Devin.

Chapter 11

THURSDAY, APRIL 6, 1865
Sayler's Creek, near Jetersville, Virginia
Late Afternoon

L EE KNOWS THAT HIS FIGHTING FORCE is splintered. Near a country estate called Lockett's Farm, the Jamestown Road crosses over Big Sayler's Creek and Little Sayler's Creek at a place called Double Bridges. There are, as the name implies, two narrow bridges. The military wagons must all funnel into a narrow line and cross one at a time.

Grant's army is now in sight. In the Confederates' attempt to rush across the bridges, the wagons become tangled. Horses and mules balk in their traces, sensing the panic and confused by the noise. One of the bridges actually collapses from the weight, and the Confederate advance comes to an abrupt halt.

Within minutes, the Union attacks. Sweeping down from the high ground, General Meade's infantry pounces on the terrified Confederates, who abandon their wagons and race into the woods on foot.

The Confederate infantry waits a few hundred yards ahead of

An Alfred Waud battlefield sketch of a scene during the Battle of Sayler's Creek. Waud, an artist who worked for Harper's Weekly, *provided many of the Civil War illustrations used in that publication.*

the chaos, watching. Four thousand of Lee's troops stand shoulder to shoulder, ready to meet the Union attack.

At first, the Confederate infantry line holds. But under heavy Union artillery fire, the men begin to fall back.

They must make a mile-long retreat over open ground that offers almost no cover. The rebel infantrymen topple the wagons that made it across the bridges, using them as cover. The sun cannot set quickly enough for these men. With 10,000 Union troops almost on top of them, darkness is the rebels' only hope.

But night does not come soon enough, and the fighting begins.

The Confederates take terrible losses. Artillery shells and bullets strike any man who dares to stand still. Many soldiers quit the war right then and there, convinced that this endless wave of blue is unbeatable.

Letters and memoirs of Confederate soldiers will reflect this dreadful campaign. "At three o'clock in the afternoon," one Confederate soldier will remember, "we reached Sayler's Creek, a small creek that at the time had overflowed its banks from the continuous rains of the past few days, giving the appearance of a small river. We halted a few minutes, then waded across this stream and took our positions on the rising ground one hundred yards beyond."

The hill is grassy, but the site of the Confederate stand is toward the back of the rise, under the cover of broom sedge and pine shrubs. Now the rebels hold the high ground. Any force attacking Lee's army will be exposed to fire while wading Sayler's Creek. If the men get across safely, they will then have to fight their way uphill to the rebel positions.

At five thirty, the Union artillery opens fire on the grassy hill from just four hundred yards away. The rebels have no artillery of their own and cannot fire back.

The shelling lasts twenty minutes. Under cover of that heavy fire, long blue lines of Union infantry wade the creek and slowly march up the hill. The Confederates do not retreat. Instead, they lie flat on the ground, muskets pointed at the stream of blue uniforms picking their way up the grassy slope. A Confederate major steps boldly in front of the line and walks the entire length, exposing himself to fire as he reminds the rebels that no one is allowed to shoot until ordered to do so. He later recalls the instruction: "That when I said 'ready' they must all rise, kneeling on the right knee; that when I said 'aim' they must all aim about the knees of the advancing line; and that when I said 'fire' they must all fire together."

Everything, as one officer notes, is as "still as the grave." The advancing line of blue moves forward, slowly ascending the hill. Some of the men wave white handkerchiefs, mocking the Confederates, jeering that they should surrender. But the rebels say nothing.

"Ready!" comes the cry from the Confederate lines.

A unit of Union artillery.

"The men rose, all together, like a piece of mechanism, kneeling on their right knees and their faces set with an expression that meant—everything," a Confederate officer will write.

On the cry of "Aim!" a line of horizontal musket barrels points directly at the blue wall. Then: "Fire!"

"I have never seen such an effect, physical and moral, produced by the utterance of one word," marvels the Confederate major. "The enemy seemed to have been totally unprepared for it."

The front row of Union soldiers falls in bloody chaos. The second line turns and runs down the hill.

In that instant, the Confederate force is overcome by righteous indignation. The memory of that hard overnight march in the rain, the starvation, the craziness brought on by exhaustion—all of it blends into a single moment of fury. The rebels leap to their feet and chase after the bluecoats.

The Union soldiers gather themselves. They stop, turn, and fire. Knowing they are outgunned, the Confederates retreat back to their positions, only to be surrounded as the Union force quickly counterattacks.

And this time Union soldiers sprint up the hill, overrunning the Confederate positions. The fighting becomes hand-to-hand. The battle degenerates into butchery and a confused struggle of personal conflicts. "I saw numbers of men kill each other with bayonets and the butts of muskets, and even bite each other's throats and ears and noses, rolling on the ground like wild beasts," one Confederate officer will write.

An illustration showing close combat between Union and Confederate infantry soldiers that appeared in Harper's New Monthly Magazine.

Robert E. Lee has spent the afternoon on horseback trying to find his own army. He sits astride Traveller, looking down from a distant ridgeline. "The disaster which had overtaken the army was in full view," one of his officers will later write. "Teamsters with their teams and dangling traces, retreating infantry without guns, many without hats, a harmless mob, with massive columns of the enemy moving orderly on."

This "harmless mob," Lee realizes, is his own Army of Northern Virginia.

"My God," says a horrified Lee. "Has the army been dissolved?"

Although the event will be little remembered in history,

witnesses will swear they have never seen more suffering or such desperate fighting as during the final moments of the Battle of Sayler's Creek.

———————◆◆✕◆◆———————

Night falls, and so ends what will come to be known as the Black Thursday of the Confederacy. Half of Lee's army is gone. All of his remaining generals, except Pete Longstreet, think the situation is hopeless. Lee continues to plan, still looking for a way to save his army and get to the Carolinas. Yet even he is devastated. "A few more Sayler's Creeks and it will all be over," he sighs.

Still, Lee cannot bring himself to utter the one word he dreads most: *surrender.*

An Alfred Waud sketch of Confederate troops with their muskets held butt upward to signal surrender.

Chapter
12

FRIDAY, APRIL 7, 1865
City Point, Virginia
Dawn

LINCOLN IS DESPERATE FOR NEWS from the front. The time away from the White House was meant to be a working vacation, and it has clearly revived him. The incredible sadness he has carried for so long is gone, replaced by serene joy. Mary Lincoln has joined her husband at City Point, bringing with her a small group of guests from Washington. The mood in the nation's capital has turned festive since the fall of Richmond. Mary and her guests plan to visit Richmond in the morning; the burned-out husk of a city has become a tourist attraction. Lincoln will stay behind on the riverboat and tend to the war. Still, he is glad for the company. He tells jokes and makes small talk, all the while wondering when the next telegram from General Grant will arrive.

Early on the morning of April 7, just hours after the battle at Sayler's Creek, Lincoln receives the news for which he's been waiting. Grant's telegram states that Sheridan has ridden over the

A Mathew Brady portrait of Mary Todd Lincoln taken in 1861.

battlefield, counting Confederate dead and captured, particularly the many top Confederate generals now in Union custody. "If the thing is pressed," Grant quotes Sheridan as saying, "I think Lee will surrender."

Lincoln telegraphs his heartfelt reply: "Let the thing be pressed."

Chapter 13

PALM SUNDAY, APRIL 9, 1865
Appomattox Court House

THE END HAS COME. The Army of Northern Virginia is cornered in a quiet little village called Appomattox Court House. Lee's 8,000 men are surrounded on three sides by Grant's 60,000. After escaping Sayler's Creek, the rebels reached Farmville, only to be attacked again. Forced to flee before they could finish eating their rations, they raced across High Bridge. The Union army crossed right behind them. Grant was then able to get ahead and block Lee's path to the Carolinas.

Lee's final great hope for a breakout came the previous night. He had entrusted his toughest general, John Gordon from Georgia, with punching a hole in the Union lines. The attack began at five P.M. Three hours later, after encountering wave after never-ending wave of blue-clad soldiers—too many for his men to beat back— Gordon sent word back to Lee that he had "fought my corps to a frazzle."

In other words, Gordon could not break through.

Lee's proud shoulders slumped as he received the news. "There is nothing left for me to do but go and see General Grant," he said. The man who had succeeded his entire life, excelling at everything and failing at nothing, was beaten. "I would rather die a thousand deaths," he said.

Union soldiers standing in front of the courthouse at
Appomattox Court House, April 1865.

Lieutenant General Grant, portrait by the famous illustrator N. C. Wyeth. Wyeth is best known for his illustrations in Treasure Island, Robinson Crusoe, *and other adventure and fantasy books.*

Wearing his dress uniform, polished black boots, and clean red sash, Lee rides forth. A spectacular ceremonial sword is buckled around his waist. He expects to meet Grant once he crosses over the Union lines, there to surrender his sword and be taken prisoner.

Lee and a small group of aides ride to a spot between the Union and Confederate lines. They halt their horses in the middle of the country lane and wait for Grant to meet them.

And they wait. And they wait some more. It becomes increasingly obvious that the Union forces are preparing for battle. Lee can see it in the way the artillery crews are positioning their cannons toward his lines.

And Grant is miles away, suffering from a severe migraine headache. Lee sits astride his horse, painfully vulnerable to a sniper's bullet despite his flag of truce. After about two hours with no response, Lee sees a Union soldier riding out. The soldier informs Lee that the attack will be launched in a few moments. For his own safety, Lee must return to the Confederate lines.

Soon the boom of artillery breaks the morning quiet. Lee jots a quick note intended for Grant and hands it to a Confederate soldier, who gallops toward the Union lines under a white flag. Lee requests that the attack be postponed until Grant can be located.

The Union colonel in charge tells the soldier that he does not have the authority to halt the attack. It will go forward as planned.

As the soldier gallops back to Lee, small patrols of Union infantry march to the front and prepare to probe the Confederate lines for vulnerability.

Lee writes another letter to Grant, asking for "a suspension of the hostilities pending the adjustment of the terms of the surrender of this army."

Even as fighting threatens to break out all around him, Lee waits, unruffled. But when the first wave of Union infantry is just a hundred yards away, Lee has no choice but to find safety. With a reluctant tug on Traveller's reins, he turns back toward his men. Moments later, he is stopped. A Union messenger tells Lee that his letter has not found Grant, but it has found General George Meade, who has ordered a sixty-minute truce.

Finally, at twelve fifteen, a lone Union officer and his Confederate escort arrive to see Lee. The officer, a colonel named Babcock, delivers a letter into Lee's hands:

> General R. E. Lee,
> Commanding C.S. Armies:
>
> Your note of this date is of but this moment (11:50 a.m.) received. In consequence of my having passed from the Richmond and Lynchburg road to the Farmville and Richmond road, I am at this writing about four miles west of Walker's church, and will push forward to the front for the purpose of meeting you. Notice sent on this road where you wish the interview to take place will meet me.
>
> Very respectfully, your obedient servant
> U. S. Grant
> Lieutenant-General

With a mixture of sadness and relief, Lee and his three aides ride past the Union lines. The Sunday afternoon is unusually quiet after so many days and years of war.

As directed in Grant's letter, Lee sends his aide Colonel Charles Marshall up the road to find a meeting place. Marshall settles on a simple home. By a great twist of fate, the house belongs to a grocer named Wilmer McLean, who moved to Appomattox Court House to escape the war. A cannonball had landed in his fireplace during the first Battle of Bull Run, at the very start of the conflict. By flee-ing to a quieter corner of Virginia, he had hoped to protect his family from harm.

But the Civil War has once again found Wilmer McLean. He

and his family are asked to leave the house. Soon, Lee marches up the front steps and takes a seat in the parlor. Again, he waits.

At one thirty, after a half hour, Lee hears a large group of horsemen galloping up to the house. Moments later, General Grant walks into the parlor. He wears a private's uniform; it is missing a button. On his shoulders he has pinned shoulder boards bearing the three stars of a lieutenant general. He has been wearing the same clothes since Wednesday night, and they are now spattered with mud from his thirty-five-mile ride this morning.

The Wilmer McLean farmhouse at Appomattox Court House, April 1865.

Removing his yellow cloth riding gloves, Grant steps forward and shakes Lee's hand.

As Grant's generals and staff—among them Sheridan and Custer—file into the room and stand to one side, Lee's aides gather behind their leader.

The generals talk about Mexico, where both men fought on the same side, recalling names of long-ago battles like Churubusco and Veracruz. Grant finds the conversation so pleasant that he momentarily forgets the reason for their meeting. Lee is the one to take the initiative.

"I suppose, General Grant, that the object of our present meeting is fully understood," he says. "I asked to see you to ascertain upon what terms you would receive the surrender of my army."

Grant calls for his order book, a thin volume of yellow paper with carbon sheets. He stares at a page, composing the sequence of words that will most amicably end the war. Lee watches as Grant writes out his terms in pen.

When he is finished, Grant hands the book over to Lee.

Lee digests the words in silence. The kind and generous terms are remarkable. Lee will not even have to surrender his sword. The meaning is simple: Put down your guns and go home. Let's rebuild the nation together. This is President Lincoln's vision, and Grant agrees with it.

As Lee rides back to his lines, the Army of Northern Virginia spontaneously gathers on both sides of the road. Lee fights back tears as his men call out to him. His dissolved army will soon turn over their guns and battle flags. This is their last chance to show their great love and respect for their leader. "Men," he calls out to them, "we have fought this war together and I have done the best I can for you."

Each group cheers as Lee approaches, only to give in to sorrow and break down in sobs as he rides past.

Meanwhile, the reconciliation is beginning. Confederate and Union officers are renewing old friendships. "They went over, had a pleasant time with their old friends, and brought some of them back with them when they returned," Grant will write twenty years later, recalling that the

A Currier & Ives lithograph of Lee's surrender to Grant. This illustration is historically inaccurate. In reality, the two men sat at separate small tables at opposite ends of the room.

McLean household became their meeting place that night. The men swapped stories of their lives and remembrances of battles won and lost. "Here the officers of both armies came in great numbers, and seemed to enjoy the meeting as much as though they had been friends separated for a long time while fighting under the same flag.

"For the time being it looked very much as if all thought of the war had escaped their minds."

But the war is not so easily forgotten by others. Unknown to all these men who risked their lives to fight great battles—men who deserved to enjoy the peace—plans will soon be hatched to seek revenge for the Union victory.

PART TWO

THE CONSPIRACY TO ASSASSINATE

Chapter 14

MONDAY, APRIL 10, 1865
Washington, D.C.
Night

T HE WAR IS OVER! Strictly speaking, this is not true. Only Lee and his army have surrendered. The Confederacy, though dying, is not yet dead. Confederate president Jefferson Davis and his government have not been captured. And General Joseph E. Johnston's army in North Carolina is still fighting Major General William T. Sherman's army. But after four long years, and more than 600,000 dead from both sides, the people of the North can be forgiven the joy and excitement that now floats through the air.

Complete strangers shake one another's hands like long-lost friends. Crowds snake toward the White House, holding torches to light the way. The city is also lit by gas lamps atop the Capitol dome. For the first time since the beginning of the war, the building that Lincoln considers the most important in Washington glows. The

*A July 1863 photograph of the Capitol building
under construction, southeast view.*

people of Washington, overcome by news of the war's end, hope to glimpse their president on this historic night. Perhaps, if they are very lucky, he will give one of the speeches for which he has become so famous.

The crowd of more than 2,000 comes to a halt on the front lawn of the White House, waiting for Lincoln to show himself from the windows of the second-floor residence. When he doesn't appear right away, they cry out for him. At first it's just a few random

An illustration of the White House in the 1870s.

shouts. Soon they roar as one: "Lincoln," the people cry. "Speech!"

Lincoln comes to the window, smiling and holding up a hand in acknowledgment. "I am very greatly rejoiced to find that an occasion has occurred so pleasurable that the people cannot restrain themselves," he jokes.

He hears the cheers and the loud cry in unison of "Speech."

Lincoln would like to make one. But his thoughts are half formed, and the words not yet written. Instead of telling the crowd what's on his mind, Lincoln smiles his easy grin. If you want to hear a speech, Lincoln yells to the crowd, please come back tomorrow night.

Spying the Navy Yard brass band taking shelter under the White House eaves, he calls out a request: "I always thought that 'Dixie' was one of the best tunes I ever heard. Our adversaries over the way, I know, have attempted to appropriate it. But I insist that yesterday we fairly captured it." He then directs the band to "favor us with a performance."

As the musicians strike up the Confederate anthem and the crowd sings and claps to that old familiar rhythm, Lincoln slips back into the White House and starts writing the last speech he will ever give.

Chapter
15

MONDAY, APRIL 10, 1865
Washington, D. C.
Night

JOHN WILKES BOOTH PICKS UP HIS GUN.

One mile down Pennsylvania Avenue, the twenty-six-year-old actor stands alone at a shooting range. In his fist he cradles a derringer, the sort of pint-size pistol favored by ladies and card-sharps.

John Wilkes Booth is one of twelve children born to his flamboyant actor father, Junius Brutus Booth. Booth's father abandoned his first wife and two children in England and fled to America with eighteen-year-old Mary Ann Holmes, who became Booth's mother. Booth was often lost in the confusion of the chaotic household. His upbringing was hectic, to say the least.

Booth's hatred for Lincoln, and his deep belief in the institution of slavery, fused into a rage after the president issued the Emancipation Proclamation in 1863. In August 1864, when a bacterial infection known as erysipelas sidelined him from the stage, Booth used his time to recruit a gang that would help him kidnap Lincoln. First he contacted his old friends Michael O'Laughlen and Samuel Arnold. They met at Barnum's City Hotel in Baltimore, and after several drinks, Booth asked them if they would join his conspiracy. Both men agreed. From there, Booth began adding others, select-ing them based on expertise with weapons, physical fitness, and knowledge of southern Maryland's back roads and waterways. The list eventually grew to include Lewis Powell, David Herold, John H. Surratt, Jr., and the carriage repairer George Atzerodt. Booth literally bought their loyalty, giving them food, clothing, and drink. And because he was a famous actor, they quickly came to enjoy their elevated status as friends of John Wilkes Booth.

In October 1864, Booth traveled to the Canadian city of Mon-treal, where he met with agents of Jefferson Davis. The Confeder-ate president had set aside more than $1 million in gold to pay for acts of espionage and intrigue against the Union and kept a portion of the money in Canada. Booth's meeting with Davis's men not only provided funding for his conspiracy, it forged a direct bond between himself and the Confederacy. He returned with a check for $1,500, along with a letter of

John Wilkes Booth's derringer.

Samuel Arnold.   *John Surratt.*   *Michael O'Laughlen.*

introduction that would allow him to meet more prominent Southern sympathizers in Maryland who would become key players in his plan. Booth knew that without their help, his chances of successfully smuggling Lincoln out of Washington and into the Deep South were nonexistent.

Now, with the surrender of Lee and the Army of Northern Virginia, Booth's plans have changed.

------◆◆◆◆◆------

Booth fires the derringer. Then he examines where the bullet hit the target. Satisfied, he reloads. Since Lee's surrender, Booth's mood is a mixture of rage and despondence. That's why he's at the range. He has a major decision to make. Shooting helps him think.

Lewis Powell/Payne.   *George Atzerodt.*   *David Herold.*

Booth is considering a new scheme. But it is so crazy, so down-right impossible, that he isn't certain his fellow conspirators will go along with it.

Booth fires at the bull's-eye.

The derringer is less than six inches long and made of brass, with a two-inch barrel. It launches a single large .44-caliber ball instead of a bullet and is accurate only at close range.

Booth loads his gun for one last shot, still plotting his next course of action.

Richmond is gone, and with it the Confederate leadership. The "secesh" community—those Southern secessionist sympathizers living a secret life in the nation's capital—is in disarray. There's no one to offer guidance.

Until now, Booth has taken orders from Jefferson Davis. But because he no longer has a way to communicate with Davis, Booth must decide for himself what is wrong and what is right. And Lincoln is still the enemy. He always will be.

So if Booth is no longer a kidnapper, how will he wage war? This is the question that has bothered him all night.

Chapter 16

MONDAY, APRIL 10, 1865
Washington, D. C.
Night

BOOTH'S WASHINGTON RESIDENCE is the National Hotel, on the corner of Pennsylvania Avenue and Sixth Street. Just around the corner is James Pumphrey's stable, where he often rents a horse. The actor feels perfectly at home at Pumphrey's, for the owner is known to be a Confederate sympathizer.

I am the man who will end Abraham Lincoln's life. That thought motivates Booth as he walks. He returns to the idea over and over again. *This is wartime. Killing the enemy is no more illegal than capturing him.*

An 1860 illustration by A. Meyer of Pennsylvania Avenue in Washington, D.C. The National Hotel is on the left.

It occurs to him that no American president has ever been assassinated. *I will be the first man to ever kill a president.* He is now even more dazzled by his own violent plan.

Booth turns onto C Street and then out of the cold, wet night into James Pumphrey's stable. A quick glance around the stalls shows that most of the horses are already rented out for the evening. Pumphrey may be a Confederate sympathizer, but he has no qualms about making money off this night of Union celebration.

Pumphrey is an acquaintance of twenty-year-old John Surratt, the messenger instrumental in ensuring that Booth's operation is fully funded by the Confederacy. Surratt travels frequently between Canada, the South, New York City, and Washington, arranging deals for everything from guns to medicine.

Mary Surratt.

When he is not traveling, John Surratt lives in a boardinghouse on Sixth and H Streets that is run by his mother, Mary Surratt. Like her son, the attractive forty-year-old widow is a Confederate sympathizer who has been involved with spying and smuggling weapons.

Washington, D.C., with its federal employees and Union loyalties, is a city whose citizens are all too prone to report any conversation that suggests pro-Confederate leanings, making it a dangerous place for people like Mary Surratt and John Wilkes Booth. Her boardinghouse and Pumphrey's stable are among the few places where they can speak their minds.

It would seem natural that Booth tell the others about

his new plan. They might have insights into the best possible routes of escape once the group has left the city.

The only way out of Washington, D.C., is on a boat or over a bridge.

The first route is over the Georgetown Aqueduct, a mile and a half northwest of the White House. The second is Long Bridge, south of the White House. The third is Benning's Bridge, on the east side of town. And the last one is the Navy Yard Bridge, on Eleventh Street.

But Booth has already made up his mind: the Navy Yard Bridge. The other three lead into Virginia, with its many roadblocks and Union soldiers. But the Navy Yard Bridge will take him into the quiet backcountry of Maryland, home to smugglers and back roads. The only problem is that sentries man the bridge and no traffic is allowed in or out of Washington after nine P.M.

Booth walks up to Ford's Theatre on Tenth Street. Although he performed at Ford's one night in mid-March, his theater appearances are few and far between these days. He still, however, has his mail sent to Ford's, and his buggy is parked in a space behind the theater that was specially created for him by a carpenter and stagehand named Ned Spangler. Booth uses Spangler often for favors and odd jobs. Thirty-nine years old and described by friends

Ned Spangler.

as "a very good, efficient drudge," the hard-drinking Spangler often sleeps in either the theater or a nearby stable. Despite the late hour, Booth knows he will find him at Ford's.

Inside the theater, rehearsals are under way for the final performance of the farce *Our American Cousin*. Like most actors, Booth knows it well.

Booth finds Spangler backstage, drunk, as usual. He asks the stagehand to clean up his carriage and find a buyer. Spangler is devastated—a great deal of work has gone into modifying the theater's storage space so that the carriage will fit. It's a waste for Booth to sell the carriage, and Spangler tells him so.

"I have no further use for it," Booth replies. "And anyway, I'll soon be leaving town."

Ford's Theatre is the building with five arches.
This photograph by Mathew Brady was taken between 1871 and 1880.

Chapter 17

TUESDAY, APRIL 11, 1865
Washington, D. C.
Evening

ABRAHAM LINCOLN IS SPEAKING tonight at the White House, and everyone wants to hear.

The spring air is warm and misty as the sea of humanity parades down Pennsylvania Avenue. Thousands upon thousands are on their way to hear the president.

An Alfred Waud sketch of a flag-raising ceremony in front of the White House in 1861.

John Wilkes Booth leans against a tall tree as the crowd surges by. He is close enough that Lincoln will be a mere pistol shot away. With him are David Herold and Lewis Powell. Herold is a former pharmacy clerk who was born and raised in Washington, D.C. Like Booth, he possesses matinee-idol good looks. But he is more educated and rugged. Herold received his pharmacy training from Georgetown College, and he is fond of spending his leisure time with a rifle in his hand, hunting animals. It was John Surratt who introduced the two, four months earlier. Since then, Herold has been an impassioned and committed member of Booth's team.

Lewis Powell—who also goes by the name Lewis Payne—is a twenty-year-old who served as a Confederate soldier and spy before joining Booth's cause. The youngest in Booth's group, Powell is tall, powerfully built, and very handsome—except that his face is misshapen on one side, the result of a mule's kick. He is also a dangerous young man, with a violent, quick temper.

Booth hasn't told the others that the plan has changed from kidnapping to assassination. He brought them along to hear Lincoln's speech, hoping that some phrase will fill them with rage. When it does, Booth will let them in on his new plan.

Soon Lincoln stands before an open second-story window, a piece of paper in one hand.

The mere sight of Lincoln thrills the crowd. The applause rolls on and on and on, continuing even as Lincoln tries to speak.

Looking out into the audience, he prepares to tell them about the task ahead and how the ability to trust the Southern states to peacefully rejoin the Union will be as great a challenge to the nation as the war itself. It is, in fact, a downbeat speech, almost an informal State of the Union address, designed to undercut the revelry and prepare the country for years of more pain and struggle.

The president begins gently. "We meet this evening not in sorrow, but in gladness of heart," Lincoln says. He thanks General Grant and the army for their struggle, and promises to have a national day of celebration very soon, with a great parade through Washington.

The speech is so long and so unexciting that people in the audience begin shifting their feet and then lowering their heads and slipping away into the night, off to search for a real celebration. Booth stays, of course. He doesn't want to miss a single word. He listens as Lincoln talks of extending voting rights to literate blacks and those who fought for the Union.

Booth seethes at the outrageous notion that slaves be considered equal citizens of the United States. He points to the Colt Navy revolver on Powell's hip. The Colt has more than enough pop to kill Lincoln from such close range. "Shoot him now," Booth commands Powell. "Put a bullet in his head right this instant."

A soldier in a Confederate uniform holding a Colt Navy revolver in his right hand and a Bowie knife in his left.

But Powell refuses to draw his weapon. He is afraid of offending Booth but even more terrified of this mob, which would surely tear him limb from limb.

"*I'll* put him through," Booth sneers, planting another seed about assassination in the minds of Powell and Herold. "By God, I'll put him through."

Then Booth spins around and fights his way out of the crowd. Twenty-four hours ago, he was still thinking of ways to kidnap the president. Now Lincoln's speech has reinforced his change of plans. He will shoot Abraham Lincoln dead.

A March 6, 1865, photograph of Abraham Lincoln, one of the last photographs taken of the president. The stress of the war shows in his worn features.

Chapter 18

TUESDAY, APRIL 11, 1865
Washington, D.C.
Night

THERE HAVE BEEN THREATS against Lincoln's life since he was first elected president.

The first was the Baltimore Plot, in 1861, in which a group known as the Knights of the Golden Circle planned to shoot Lincoln as he traveled to Washington for the inauguration. In a strange twist, many newspapers mocked Lincoln for the way he eluded the assassins by wearing a cheap disguise as he snuck into Washington. His enemies made much of the deception, labeling Lincoln a coward and refusing to believe that such a plot existed in the first place.

The Baltimore Plot taught Lincoln a powerful lesson about public perception. Since that day, he has adopted a veneer of unshakable courage. Now he moves freely throughout Washington. In 1862 he began having military protection beyond the walls of the White House, but it was only late in 1864, as the war wound down and the threats became more real, that Washington's Metropolitan

Police assigned a select group of armed officers to protect him. Two remain at his side from eight A.M. to four P.M. Another stays until midnight, when a fourth man takes the graveyard shift, posting himself outside Lincoln's bedroom or following the president through the White House when he cannot sleep.

Ward H. Lamon.

The truth is that Lincoln, despite what he says, secretly believes he will die in office. His closest friend and security adviser, the barrel-chested Ward Hill Lamon, preaches regularly to Lincoln about the need for improved security measures. As evidence of the need, there is a packet nestled in a small cubby of Lincoln's upright desk. It is marked, quite simply, "Assassination." Inside are more than eighty death threats.

"The first one or two made me a little uncomfortable," Lincoln has admitted to an artist who came to paint his portrait, "but they have ceased to give me any apprehension."

Rather than dwell on death, Lincoln prefers to live life on his own terms. "If I am killed I can die but once," he is fond of saying. "But to live in constant dread is to die over and over again."

Normally, because of the memories it will

An engraving by William Sartain of Abraham Lincoln and his family in the White House. From left to right: Thomas, Abraham, Robert Todd, and Mary Todd.

raise in his wife of the deaths of their sons Edward, from tuberculosis, and Willie, from typhoid fever, Lincoln does not talk about death with Mary present. But on this night, surrounded by friends and empowered by the confessional tone of the speech, he can't help himself.

"I had a dream the other night, which has haunted me since," he admits soulfully.

"You frighten me," Mary cries.

Lincoln will not be stopped. He tells her that, ten days ago, he

LITTLE "TAD" LINCOLN.

An illustration over a Mathew Brady photograph of William "Willie" Lincoln, who died in 1862 at the age of eleven. The photograph was taken shortly before his death.

A photograph of Thomas "Tad" Lincoln on horseback taken between 1860 and 1865. Tad would die of heart failure at the age of eighteen in 1871.

went to bed late. That night, he had stood alone on the top deck of a steamboat called the *River Queen*, watching Grant's big guns shell the Confederate defenders of Petersburg.

Lieutenant General Ulysses S. Grant, 1865.

> I had been waiting for important dispatches from the front. I could not have been long in bed when I fell into a slumber, for I was weary. I soon began to dream.
>
> There seemed to be a deathlike stillness about me. Then I heard subdued sobs, as if a number of people were weeping. I thought I left my bed and wandered downstairs. There the silence was broken by the same pitiful sobbing, but the mourners were invisible. I went from room to room. No living person was in sight, but the same mournful sounds of distress met me as I passed along. It was light in all the rooms. Every object was familiar to me. But where were all the people who were grieving as if their hearts would break? I was puzzled and alarmed. What could be the meaning of all this?
>
> Determined to find the cause of a state of things so mysterious and shocking, I kept on until I arrived in the East Room, which I entered. There I was met with a sickening surprise. Before me was a catafalque, on which rested a corpse wrapped in funeral vestments. Around it were stationed soldiers who were acting as guards. And there were a throng of people, some gazing mournfully upon the corpse, whose face was

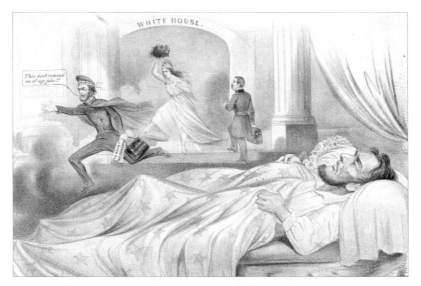

This Currier & Ives drawing, Abraham's dream!— "Coming events cast their shadows before," *portrays the president tormented by nightmares of defeat in the election of 1864.*

covered, others weeping pitifully. "Who is dead in the White House?" I demanded of one of the soldiers. "The President," was the answer. "He was killed by an assassin." Then came a loud burst of grief from the crowd.

Mary doesn't want to hear. "That is horrid," she wails. "I wish you had not told it."

"Well, it was only a dream, Mary," he chides her. "Let us say no more about it."

A moment later, seeing the uneasiness in the room, Lincoln adds, "Don't you see how it will all turn out? In this dream it was not me, but some other fellow that was killed."

His words cheer no one, especially not Mary.

Chapter 19

WEDNESDAY, APRIL 12, 1865
Washington, D.C.
Morning

AFTER A NIGHT OF RESTLESS SLEEP and a light breakfast, Booth walks the streets of Washington, his mind filled with the many strands of his unfinished plan. The longer he walks, the more it all comes together.

It is the morning after Lincoln's speech and the third day since Lee's surrender.

Booth frames every action through the prism of the dramatic, a trait that comes from being born and raised in an acting household. As he builds the assassination scheme in his head, layer by layer, everything is designed to make him the star performer. This will be the biggest assassination plot ever, and his commanding performance will guarantee an eternity of recognition.

He knows there will be an audience. By the morning after Lincoln's speech, Booth has decided to shoot the president inside a theater, the place where Booth feels most comfortable. Lincoln is known to attend the theater frequently.

Booth walks faster, energized by the awareness that he has much to do.

He must find out when Lincoln will be attending the theater and which one. He must find out which play is being performed, so that he can select just the right moment in the show for the execution—a moment with few actors onstage, if possible. The escape plan is to gallop out of Washington on horseback and disappear into the loving arms of the South, where friends and allies and even complete strangers who have heard of his daring deed will see that he makes it safely to Mexico.

But that's not all.

There are rumors that General Grant will be in town. If he attends the theater with Lincoln, which is a very real possibility, Booth can kill the two most important causes of the South's fall within seconds.

And yet Booth wants even more. The team he put together for the kidnapping will do whatever he asks. Rather than just kill Lincoln and Grant, he now plans to do nothing less than undertake a top-down destruction of the government of the United States of America.

Vice President Andrew Johnson is an obvious target. He is first in line to the presidency, lives at a nearby hotel, and is completely unguarded. Like all Confederate sympathizers, Booth views the Tennessee politician as a turncoat for siding with the Union and Lincoln.

Secretary of State William H. Seward, whose oppressive policies toward the South have long made him a target of Confederate anger, is on Booth's list as well.

The deaths of Lincoln, Grant, Johnson, and Seward should be more than enough to cause chaos in the government and begin to avenge the South.

To Lewis Powell, the former Confederate spy who watched Lincoln's speech with Booth, will go the task of killing Secretary Seward, who, at age sixty-three, is currently bedridden after a near-fatal carriage accident. He has no chance of leaping from the bed to elude a surprise attack.

Powell's job should be as simple as sneaking into the Seward home, shooting the sleeping secretary in his bed, then galloping away to join Booth for a life of sunshine and easy living in Mexico. For the job of killing Johnson, Booth selects a drifter named George Atzerodt, a German carriage repairer

Vice President
Andrew Johnson.

William H. Seward was ambitious and powerful. His opposition to slavery made him one of Booth's targets.

with an unhealthy complexion who drinks a lot. He was brought into the plot for his encyclopedic knowledge of the smuggling routes from Washington, D.C., into the Deep South. Booth suspects that Atzerodt may be unwilling to go along with the new plot. Should that be the case, Booth has a foolproof plan in mind to blackmail Atzerodt into cooperating.

Chapter 20

THURSDAY, APRIL 13, 1865
Washington, D.C.

G ENERAL ULYSSES S. GRANT and his wife, Julia, arrive in Washington at dawn. He is eager to push on to New Jersey to see their four children, but Secretary of War Edwin Stanton has specifically requested that the general visit the capital and handle a number of war-related issues. Grant's plan is to get in and get out within twenty-four hours, with as little fuss as possible. With him are his aide Lieutenant Colonel Horace Porter and two sergeants to manage the Grants' luggage.

Julia Grant.

Little does Grant know that an adoring Washington, D.C., is waiting to wrap its arms around him. "As we reached our destination that bright morning in our boat," Julia later exclaimed, "every gun in and near Washington

Secretary of War Edwin M. Stanton.

burst forth—and such a salvo!—all the bells rang out merry greetings, and the city was literally swathed in flags and bunting."

If anything, Grant is even more beloved than the president right now. Strangers cheer the Grants' open-air carriage on its way to the Willard Hotel, on the corner of Pennsylvania Avenue and Fourteenth Street.

The Grants have been married for more than twenty years and have endured many long separations due to military life. Julia's letters sustained Ulysses during the Mexican War, when he was a homesick young lieutenant. And Julia stood by her husband's side during the 1850s, when he was discharged from the army and failed in a succession of businesses. They are happiest in each other's company. And right now they need to get to their room and wash up before the general goes over to the War Department.

There's just one problem: the Grants don't have a reservation at the Willard Hotel.

Grant has slept so many nights in battlefield lodgings arranged for by his staff that it never crossed his mind to send a telegram asking for a room. What he wants, he tells the flustered desk clerk, is a

The Willard Hotel, photograph taken in the early 1920s.

simple bedroom with a sitting room. It's understood that Colonel Porter will need a room, too. The sergeants will bunk elsewhere.

The Willard Hotel is full. Yet to allow the famous Ulysses S. Grant to take a room at another hotel would be unthinkable.

Somehow, rooms are instantly made available. Within minutes, Julia is unpacking their suitcases. Word about their location is already flying around Washington, and bundles of congratulatory messages and flowers soon flood the desk and bedroom. Julia will spend the afternoon reading each note.

Not that General Grant cares. He just wants to get on with his business and return home. Within minutes, he and Porter meet in the lobby, then step out onto Pennsylvania Avenue for the short walk to the War Department. At first the going is easy. They are just two regular guys in uniform joining the sea of pedestrians, soldiers, and tourists. But Grant is hard to miss. Images of his bearded, expressionless face have been on the front pages of newspapers for more than a year. Soon autograph seekers and well-wishers surround him. Porter tries to push them back, protecting his general. But there are so many that Grant is swallowed by the crowd.

Just when the situation begins to border on pandemonium, the Metropolitan Police come to their rescue. Grant and Porter are soon on their way again, this time inside a carriage, with a cavalry escort.

At the War Department, Grant reads telegrams from his commanders in the field, issues appropriate orders, and takes care of a variety of administrative tasks requiring his attention. After that business is done, he meets with Lincoln at the White House. A grateful Lincoln offers his congratulations. He calls for a carriage. The two men ride around the crowded streets of Washington with the top down. The ride is Lincoln's way of giving Grant his moment in the sun after so many months of hardship.

It works. The two men are loudly cheered on every street corner.

Meanwhile, John Wilkes Booth continues to work on his conspiracy of revenge that will turn all this joy into sadness.

Lieutenant Colonel
Horace Porter.

PART THREE

LINCOLN'S LAST DAY

Lincoln's chair.

Chapter 21

FRIDAY, APRIL 14, 1865
Washington, D. C.
7 A.M.

L INCOLN AWAKENS AT SEVEN A.M. Outside the White House, the Washington weather is splendid, a sunny fifty-degree day. The president rises from his bed, slips on a pair of battered slippers, pulls on a weathered robe, and walks down a second-floor hallway to the library.

The president's favorite chair is in the exact center of the room. He sits down and opens his Bible, not because it is Good Friday, the Friday before Easter, but because starting the day reading Scripture is his lifelong habit.

Lincoln then walks down the hall to his office. His desk is mahogany, with cubbies and shelves. He can see the Potomac River clearly out the window.

Breakfast is scheduled for eight o'clock. Lincoln is eager to be downstairs because his son Robert is just back from the war and will be joining him, twelve-year-old Tad, and Mary for breakfast.

Robert Todd Lincoln, photograph taken about 1860.

Robert was in the room when Lee surrendered at Appomattox. Though Lincoln heard the story from Grant yesterday, he is eager to hear more.

Robert is just twenty-one, with a thin mustache and a captain's rank in the Union army. As Lincoln sips coffee and eats a single boiled egg—his usual breakfast—Robert describes "the stately elegant Lee" and Grant, "the small stooping shabby shy man in the muddy blue uniform, with no sword and no spurs."

When Lincoln asks what it was like to be there, his son is breathless. "Oh, it was great!" the normally articulate Robert exclaims, unable to find a more expressive way to describe the event.

Pressing business awaits Lincoln in his office, but he allows breakfast to stretch on for almost an hour. At last he stands. He is relaxed and happy, even though the stress of the war had caused him to lose so much weight that he looks like "a skeleton with clothes," in the words of one friend.

By nine A.M., President Lincoln is sitting at his desk. His workday has officially begun.

A mile down Pennsylvania Avenue, John Wilkes Booth is setting his affairs in order.

Chapter 22

FRIDAY, APRIL 14, 1865

Washington, D. C.

10 A.M.

Mary Todd Lincoln. Photograph by Nicholas H. Shepherd in 1846 or 1847.

MARY LINCOLN KNOWS that the wildly popular farce *Our American Cousin* is at Ford's Theatre. Tonight the legendary actress Laura Keene is celebrating the last night of her Washington run as her signature character Florence Trenchard. This event, Mary decides, is something not to be missed.

Thirty-eight-year-old Laura Keene is one of America's most famous actresses. She owes much of her success to *Our American Cousin*. Debuting seven years earlier in New York City, it soon became the first blockbuster play in American history. Many of the play's silly and made-up terms, like "sockdologizing" and "Dundrearyisms" (named for the befuddled character Lord Dundreary), have become part of everyday speech, and several spin-off plays featuring characters from the show have been written and performed.

Mary Lincoln is looking forward to celebrating recent Union victories by enjoying this popular comedy on a night that features Keene. At breakfast, she told the president she wanted to go to Ford's Theatre that evening. Lincoln absentmindedly said he would take care of it.

Now, between appointments, he summons a messenger. He wants a message delivered to Ford's Theatre saying that he will be in attendance this evening if the state box, the special seating section set aside for dignitaries and honored guests, is available. General Grant and his wife will be with him, he says, as will Mary.

By this time, Lincoln is overdue at the War Department. He also

Laura Keene,
photographed between
1855 and 1865.

has a cabinet meeting scheduled in just over an hour. He hurriedly steps out of the White House and walks over to see Secretary of War Stanton. Mary has made him promise to wear a shawl outside, and so he does.

Lincoln enters Stanton's office unannounced, plops down on the couch, and casually mentions that he's going to the theater that night. The words are designed to provoke a reaction—and they do.

Stanton frowns. His network of spies has told him of increasing numbers of assassination rumors over the past few days. It is impossible to tell the difference between idle threats and serious ones. Stanton thinks the president is a fool for ignoring the rumors and argues that Lincoln is risking his life.

"At least bring a guard with you," Stanton pleads, once it becomes obvious that Lincoln will not be dissuaded.

His business with Stanton concluded, Lincoln wraps his shawl tightly around his shoulders and marches back to the White House for his cabinet meeting.

The Ford's Theatre advertising poster announcing President Lincoln's presence that evening.

Chapter 23

FRIDAY, APRIL 14, 1865
Washington, D. C.
10:30 A.M.

LINCOLN'S MESSENGER MANAGES to reach Ford's Theatre at 10:30 A.M. "The president of the United States would like to formally request the state box for this evening—if it is available," the note reads.

The state box is available, so the manager, James Ford, responds immediately, barely containing his excitement. He races into his office to share the good news with his brother Harry and then barks the order for the stage carpenter to come see him at once.

Ford's may be the city's most important stage, but business has been extremely slow this week. The postwar joy means that Washington's theatergoers are making merry on the streets, not inside a theater. But now, with word that the president will be in the audience, the night should be a sellout. James wants to be sure that the state box is exactly as Lincoln prefers it.

Inside the theater, three seating levels face the stage. Gas lamps light the auditorium until the curtain falls, when they are dimmed. The chairs are simple straight-backed cane but, inside his special state box, Lincoln likes to sit in the red upholstered rocking chair that Ford's reserves for his personal use.

Boxes on either side of the stage allow the more privileged patrons to look straight down onto the actors. The state box is almost on

The interior of the reconstructed Ford's Theatre, now a museum and historic site. The state box where the president sat is on the right, draped in flags.

the stage itself—so close that if Lincoln were to impulsively rise from his rocking chair and leap down into the actors' midst, the distance traveled would be twelve feet.

On this night, with the Lincolns present, red, white, and blue bunting is draped over the railing and a portrait of George Washington faces out. The managers are doing all they can to make this an especially festive occasion.

———◆•✕•◆———

At about the same time Lincoln's messenger is handing James Ford the president's note, John Wilkes Booth marches into Ford's Theatre to pick up his mail.

Booth is in the office, gathering a bundle of letters, when stage carpenter James J. Gifford bounds into the room. When the theater manager shares the exciting news about the Lincolns, Gifford is thrilled. Booth, pretending not to hear, stares down at his mail as if he is studying the return addresses. He grins, though he does not mean to. He calms himself, makes small talk with Ford, then says his good-byes and wanders out into the sunlight. Booth sits on the front step, half reading his mail and laughing aloud at his sudden good fortune.

Booth knows that he will kill Lincoln tonight and in this very theater. Now he has to finalize his plans. The twofold challenge he faces is the traditional assassin's plight: find the most efficient path into the state box and then find the perfect escape route from the theater.

The cast and crew at Ford's treat Booth like family. His eccentricities are chalked up to his status as a famous actor. So, as Booth rises to his feet and wanders back into the theater to plan the attack, it never crosses anyone's mind to ask what he's doing. It's just John being John.

John Wilkes Booth prowls Ford's Theatre alone, thinking of how he will accomplish the assassination and make his escape. His journey takes him up the back stairs to the state box, where he steps inside and looks down at the stage. A music stand provides an unlikely burst of inspiration. He lifts it, nervous but elated, knowing how he will make use of it tonight. By the time he is done, Booth has come up with a bold—and brilliant—plan.

Two Ford's Theatre tickets for the performance the night Lincoln was assassinated.

Chapter 24

FRIDAY, APRIL 14, 1865
Washington, D. C.
11 A.M.

GENERAL GRANT WALKS TO THE WHITE HOUSE for the cabinet meeting. That morning an invitation to attend the theater arrived from Mary Lincoln. He feels obligated to go. Julia Grant, who thinks Mary Lincoln is unstable and a gossip, has bluntly refused. General Grant is caught in the middle and has not discovered a solution.

The two soldiers standing guard at the White House gate snap to attention as their general in chief arrives. Grant tosses them a return salute, never breaking stride as he continues on to the front door.

The doorman nods graciously as Grant steps inside, moving past the police bodyguard and a rifle-bearing soldier. Then it's up the stairs to Lincoln's second-floor office, where another soldier stands guard. Soon Grant is seated in Lincoln's cabinet meeting. Secretary of State William Seward, home recovering from his carriage accident, is represented by his son Frederick. As Lincoln leans back in his chair along the south window, the half-filled room feels more like a college debating club than a serious cabinet-level gathering. Lincoln guides the dialogue, taking no notes. As has been his habit ever since he became president, his behavior is that of a first among equals rather than the ultimate decision maker.

Before Lincoln was elected president, he was a successful lawyer. His skill for reasoned debate and ability to listen to different points of view and thoroughly examine an issue from every angle helped make him president. That is why he lets his cabinet members talk. These are strong-willed men with strong opinions. As they speak, Lincoln directs the discussion—and thinks.

The meeting is in its second hour as Grant is shown into the room, and his entrance injects a new vitality—just as Lincoln intended. The cabinet praises the general and begs to hear details of the Appomattox surrender. Grant sets the scene, describing the quaint McLean farmhouse and the way he and Lee sat together

Secretary of the Treasury Hugh McCulloch, a member of President Lincoln's cabinet.

to settle matters. He doesn't go into great detail, and he makes a point of praising Lee. The cabinet members are struck by his modesty, but they are eager for more details.

"What terms did you make for the common soldiers?" the president asks, already knowing the answer.

"To go back to their homes and families, and they would not be molested, if they did nothing more."

Grant's simple reply has the desired effect. Lincoln beams as the cabinet members nod in agreement.

"And what of the current military situation?"

Grant says that he expects word from Sherman any minute, saying that General Joe Johnston and his Confederate army in North Carolina—its last army—has finally surrendered. This, too, is met with enthusiasm around the table.

The cabinet meeting drags on. One o'clock passes. One thirty.

A messenger arrives with a note for Grant. It's from Julia, and she's not happy. Mrs. Grant wants her husband back at the Willard Hotel immediately, so that they can catch the six o'clock train to Burlington, New Jersey.

General Grant's decision has now been made for him. After years of men obeying his every order, he bows to an even greater authority than the president of the United States: his wife.

"I am sorry, Mr. President," Grant says when the cabinet meeting ends, just after one thirty. "It is certain that I will be on this afternoon's train to Burlington. I regret that I cannot attend the theater."

Lincoln tries to change Grant's mind, telling him that the people of Washington will be at Ford's to see him. But the situation is out of the general's hands. Lincoln senses that and says good-bye to his friend.

Secretary of the Navy Gideon Welles,
a member of President Lincoln's cabinet.

Chapter
25

FRIDAY, APRIL 14, 1865
Washington, D. C.

2 P.M.

BOOTH IS ON AN EMOTIONAL ROLLER COASTER as he thinks about the assassination and its consequences. He runs down his checklist of the tasks that must be done for tonight. He is dressed in dashing fashion, with tight black pants, a tailored black coat, and a black hat. The only thing he wears that isn't black are his boots—they're tan.

The first stop is Mary Surratt's boardinghouse on H Street. She is walking out the door for a trip into the country, but Booth catches her just in time. He hands her a spyglass wrapped in brown paper and tied with a string, telling her to make sure that it doesn't get wet or break and that he'll be picking it up later in the evening.

Booth then walks the five blocks to Herndon House, where Lewis Powell is in his room, lying on the bed and staring at the ceiling. He and Booth discuss the evening's plan. The trick in killing Secretary of State Seward, Booth reminds Powell, isn't the actual murder. Seward is incapable of putting up any resistance.

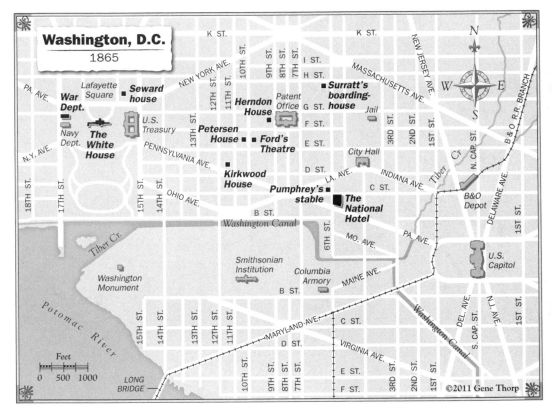

A map of Washington, D.C., showing significant landmarks in the city in 1865.

No, the hard part will be getting in and out of Seward's home. There is at least one male military nurse to protect the secretary, along with Seward's wife and three of his children. In a worst-case scenario, Powell will have to kill them all, Booth says. Powell says he has no problem with that.

Then Booth heads for Pumphrey's stable to arrange for his get-away horse. His favorite horse is already rented. So, Booth gets a compact bay mare with a white star on her forehead. Pumphrey warns Booth that the mare is extremely high-spirited. She mustn't be tied to a post if he leaves her anywhere, because she'll pull away and escape. Booth should have someone hold her reins at all times.

Booth saddles up and is on his way, walking the mare up Sixth Street to Pennsylvania Avenue. He stops at Grover's Theatre.

Booth doesn't have any business at Grover's Theatre, but theaters are safe refuges, no matter what city he's visiting. He's sure to see a friendly face.

Against Pumphrey's instructions, he ties the mare to a hitching post.

Inside Grover's, Booth walks to the manager's office. It's empty. Sitting at the desk, Booth removes a piece of paper and an envelope from the pigeonholes. He writes a letter to the editor of the *National Intelligencer* newspaper stating, in specific terms, what he is about to do.

He signs his name, then adds those of Powell, Atzerodt, and Herold. They are all members of the same company, in theatrical terms. They deserve some sort of billing—even if they might not want it.

After sealing the envelope, Booth steps outside and mounts his horse, which has managed to remain hitched. He spies fellow actor John Matthews in front of the theater. Booth leans down from his horse to hand him the envelope and gives him specific instructions to mail it the next morning. However, hedging his bets in case things go bad, Booth says he wants the letter back if he finds Matthews before ten tomorrow morning.

An 1861 panoramic view of Washington, D.C.,
looking northwest from the roof of the Capitol building.

A photograph of activity on Pennsylvania Avenue in Washington, D.C., taken in May 1865. The blurred and streaked images are the result of people, animals, and wagons moving too fast for the film to capture a clear image.

It's a petty and spiteful trick, designed to implicate Matthews, who will be onstage in the role of Richard Coyle during *Our American Cousin*. Booth had asked him to be part of the conspiracy and was turned down, repeatedly.

Now Booth hopes to get his revenge by making Matthews seem guilty by association.

Chapter 26

FRIDAY, APRIL 14, 1865
Washington, D. C.
7 P.M.

WILLIAM CROOK STANDS GUARD OUTSIDE Lincoln's office door. The twenty-six-year-old policeman and presidential bodyguard has had a long day. His replacement was supposed to relieve him three hours ago, but John Parker, as always, is late. Crook is deeply attached to Lincoln and worries about his safety. He also worries about Parker. How this drunken slob was chosen as the president's bodyguard is a great mystery, but Crook knows that the president does not involve himself in such things.

The Lincolns eat dinner with their sons, and then Crook walks the president back to the War Department to see if General Sherman has sent a telegram about General Johnston's surrender of the last Confederate army. There is no news.

As Crook returns to the White House with Lincoln, his eyes constantly scan the crowds for signs that someone means his employer harm. He remembers the advice of Ward Hill Lamon, the walrus-mustached, self-appointed head of Lincoln's security detail, who said that Lincoln should not go out at night under any circumstances. "Especially to the theater," Lamon had added.

But tonight, Lincoln is ignoring the advice, going to the theater, and it's no secret. The afternoon papers announced that he would attend *Our American Cousin* with General Grant and their wives—the Grants declined the invitation after the newspapers had been printed. Ticket sales have been brisk.

Mary was able to find two replacement

William H. Crook in a photograph taken in the 1890s.

guests, Major Henry Reed Rathbone and his fiancée, Clara Harris, who watched Lincoln's speech with Mary three nights before. Mary is deeply fond of Clara, the daughter of Senator Ira Harris of New York.

Back at the White House, Crook hears feet thudding up the

stairs. At last, John Parker ambles down the hallway, patting the bulge in his jacket to show that he is armed. He is a thirty-four-year-old former machinist from Frederick County, Virginia. Parker served a three-month term of enlistment in the Union army at the beginning of the war. After he was discharged, he rejoined his family and took a job as a policeman in September 1861, becoming one of the first 150 men hired when Washington, D.C., formed its brand-new Metropolitan Police Department.

Throughout his employment, Parker's one distinguishing trait was that of a troublemaker who somehow managed to get away with things. He has been disciplined numerous times for charges ranging from drunk and disorderly conduct to indiscipline. He was repeatedly acquitted, so Parker had no hesitation about putting his name into the pool when, late in 1864, the Metropolitan Police Department began providing White House bodyguards. It was important duty. So far, the only blemish on Parker's record while serving the president is a penchant for tardiness, as Crook knows all too well. So when Parker finally appears, several hours late for his shift, Crook is upset but not surprised.

Crook briefs Parker on the day's events, then explains that the presidential carriage will be stopping at Fourteenth and H Streets to pick up Major Rathbone and Miss Harris. The presence of two additional passengers means that there will be no room in the carriage for Parker. "You should leave fifteen minutes ahead of the president," says Crook, pointing out that Parker will have to walk to Ford's Theatre—and that he should get there before the presidential party in order to provide security the instant they arrive.

As Crook finishes, Lincoln comes to his office door. A handful of last-minute appointments have come up, and he is eager to get those out of the way so he can enjoy the weekend.

"Good night, Mr. President," Crook says.

He and the president have repeated this scene hundreds of times, with Lincoln responding in kind.

Only this time it's different.

"Good-*bye*, Crook," Lincoln replies.

The difference in Lincoln's usual parting phrase troubles William Crook, but he can't explain why.

A painting by John Chester Buttre of Lincoln in his office.

Chapter 27

FRIDAY, APRIL 14, 1865
Washington, D. C.

8 P.M.

THE FOUR CONSPIRATORS SQUEEZE into room six at the Herndon House hotel. David Herold, Lewis Powell, and George Atzerodt lounge on the chairs and perch on the edge of the bed as Booth talks them through the plan.

First, Booth tells them that the precise time of the president's assassination will be ten fifteen P.M.

Second, Booth reminds the group that the murders of Seward and Johnson must also take place at ten fifteen. The precision is vital. Booth hopes to create the illusion that Washington, D.C., is a hotbed of assassins, resulting in the sort of mass chaos that will make it easier for them all to escape.

Next comes the assignments. The job of murdering Secretary of State Seward will be a two-man affair, with Lewis Powell and David Herold working together. Powell will be the man who actually walks up to the door, finds a way to enter the house, and commits the crime. The ruse that will get him in the door is a fake bottle of medication, which Powell will claim was sent by Seward's physician.

Herold's role is to assist in the getaway. He knows Washington's back alleys and shortcuts and will guide Powell, who knows little about the city, to safety. During the murder, Herold must wait outside and hold their horses. Once Powell exits the house, the two men will leave town via the Navy Yard Bridge and rendezvous with the others in the Maryland countryside.

Secretary of State William H. Seward.

Unlike the others, Powell has actually killed before. During the war, the Alabaman fought in several major battles, was wounded at Gettysburg, successfully escaped from a prisoner-of-war camp, and worked for the Confederate Secret Service. He is a solid horseman and quick with a knife. Thanks to his military training, Powell knows the value of reconnaissance. He prepared for his part of the plot that morning by walking past Secretary of State Seward's home on Madison Place, checking for the best possible ways in and out of the building. He boldly struck up a conversation with Seward's male nurse, just to make sure the secretary was indeed at home.

George Atzerodt will act alone. Killing Vice President Andrew Johnson does not seem difficult. Though Johnson is a vigorous man, he is known to be unguarded and alone most of the time. Atzerodt is to knock on the door of his hotel room and shoot him when he answers. Atzerodt will also escape Washington over the Navy Yard Bridge, then gallop into Maryland. From there, Atzerodt's familiarity with smugglers' trails will allow him to guide the men farther south and away from Union forces.

Finally, it dawns on one very drunk George Atzerodt that the plan

has shifted from kidnapping to murder. He moonlights as a smuggler, ferrying mail, contraband, and people across the broad Potomac into Virginia. Atzerodt's role in the kidnapping was to be an act of commerce, not rebellion. He was to be paid handsomely to smuggle the bound-and-gagged Lincoln into the hands of the Confederates.

But there is no longer a Confederacy, no longer a kidnapping plot, no longer a need for a boat, and certainly no longer a need for a smuggler—at least in Atzerodt's mind. The thirty-year-old German immigrant slurs that he wants out.

Booth cannot do without Atzerodt. His boat and his knowledge of the Potomac's currents are vital to their escape. A massive manhunt will surely begin the instant Lincoln is killed. But with Atzerodt's guidance, Booth and his men can rush through rural Maryland ahead of the search parties, cross the Potomac, and follow smugglers' routes south to Mexico.

"Then *we* will do it," Booth says, nodding at Herold and Powell, never taking his eyes off the drunk German. "But what will come of you?" Booth blackmails Atzerodt, saying

Some of the belongings John Wilkes Booth took with him when he left his hotel room on April 14, 1865.

An 1874 illustration of a typical house in Washington, D.C.,
indicating it still had a small-town feel despite being the nation's capital.

he's in too deep to back out. Booth adds that if he's caught and questioned, he'll say that Atzerodt was a member of the conspiracy. Finally, Booth says that if Atzerodt still refuses to go along with the conspiracy, Booth will shoot him dead on the spot. Atzerodt sighs and nods. Murder it is.

Booth reminds the others that their post-assassination rendezvous point is the road to Nanjemoy, on the Maryland side of the Potomac at a place called Soper's Hill.

Booth shakes hands with each man. They leave one at a time and go their separate ways.

Chapter 28

FRIDAY, APRIL 14, 1865
Washington, D. C.
8:30 P.M.

BOOTH GOBBLES DOWN a quick dinner in the National Hotel's dining room. As soon as he finishes, he walks up to his room to get his weapons and gear. *Our American Cousin* starts at eight, and his plan will go into action shortly after ten P.M.

His cue is simple: there is a moment in the third act when the actor Harry Hawk, playing the part of Asa Trenchard, is the only person onstage. He utters a line that never fails to make the audience laugh. "Don't know the manners of good society, eh?" he says to the character of the busybody, Mrs. Mountchessington, who has insulted him before exiting the stage. "Well, I guess I know enough to turn you inside out, old gal—you sockdologizing old man-trap."

The instant the Ford's audience explodes into laughter, Booth will kill Lincoln. He will toss the pistol aside and then use his knife to battle his way out if cornered.

The key part of his plan is to keep moving forward at all

times—forward from the back wall of the box, forward to Lincoln's rocking chair, forward up and over the railing and down onto the stage, forward to the backstage door, forward to Maryland, and then forward all the way to Mexico, exile, and safety.

But Booth will stop for an instant in the midst of all that rapid movement. The actor in him cannot resist the chance to utter one last bold line from center stage. After leaping from the balcony Booth will stand tall and, in his best actor's voice, pronounce the Latin phrase *sic semper tyrannis*—thus always to tyrants. As Booth sees it, Lincoln is an evil tyrant who wants to destroy the South and its way of life. Booth will be the South's hero and slay the evil Lincoln.

Booth has stolen the phrase, truth be told, from the state of Virginia. It is the commonwealth's motto.

No matter. The words are perfect.

John Wilkes Booth's knife and its sheath.

Booth leaves quite a bit of evidence behind in his hotel room. Among the personal effects that authorities will later find are a broken comb, tobacco, embroidered slippers, and one very telling scrap of paper. On it are written the keys to top-secret coded Confederate messages that link him with Jefferson Davis's office in Richmond and with the million-dollar gold fund in Montreal. Finally, there is a suitcase filled with documents and letters that implicate John Surratt and, by extension, his mother, Mary.

He walks downstairs and slides his key across the front desk. "Are you going to Ford's tonight?" he asks George W. Bunker, the clerk on duty.

"No," comes the reply.

"You ought to go," Booth says with a wink on his way out the door. "There is going to be some splendid acting."

Chapter 29

FRIDAY, APRIL 14, 1865
Washington, D. C.
8:05 P.M.

Schuyler Colfax.

WOULD YOU HAVE US BE LATE?" Mary Lincoln chides her husband, standing in his office doorway. Speaker of the House Schuyler Colfax dropped by a half hour ago and was granted a few minutes of Lincoln's time. But those few minutes have stretched into half an hour. The curtain has already risen on *Our American Cousin.* Making matters worse, the Lincolns still have to pick up their theater guests. They'll be lucky to arrive at Ford's in time for the second act.

Next, former Massachusetts congressman George Ashmun wants to see Lincoln. But Mary's pleas against any additional delay finally have an effect.

Lincoln hastily pulls a card from his jacket pocket and jots a short note inviting Ashmun to return at nine in the morning.

Finally, Lincoln walks downstairs and out onto the front porch, where the presidential carriage awaits.

Personal assistant Charles Forbes helps Mary up the steps of the carriage as Lincoln says a few final words to Ashmun and Colfax, who have followed him outside. The president hears footsteps on the gravel and the familiar voice of former Illinois congressman Isaac Arnold calling his name.

Lincoln is about to follow Mary into the carriage, but he waits. Arnold was a faithful supporter of Lincoln during the war's darkest hours, and the resulting dip in the president's popularity cost Arnold his seat in the House. The least Lincoln can do is acknowledge him. He bends his head to listen as Arnold whispers in his ear.

Lincoln nods. "Excuse me now," he begs. "I am going to the theater. Come see me in the morning."

The Harris residence, at H and Fifteenth Streets, is almost right across the street from the White House, so the Lincolns are able to quickly pick up their guests.

Isaac Newton Arnold.

As the carriage travels the seven blocks to the theater, Major Rathbone, with his muttonchops and broad mustache, sits facing Lincoln, talking about his experiences in the war. Finally, they reach Ford's.

Driver Francis Burns steps down and walks the horses the final few feet to the theater. The two cavalry escorts trailing the carriage wheel their horses back to their barracks. They will return and finish their guard duty once the show ends.

It is eight twenty-five when Lincoln steps through the front door of the theater. Now rejoined by bodyguard John Parker, the Lincolns and their guests climb the stairs to their box. Onstage, the actors are more than aware that the audience is in a foul mood.

Having bought tickets in hopes of seeing Lincoln and Grant, the theatergoers have monitored the state box, only to find it empty.

So when Lincoln finally arrives, there is relief onstage. Laura Keene improvises a line that refers to Lincoln, making the audience turn toward the side of the theater in order to witness his appearance. William Withers, the orchestra director, immediately stops the show's music and instructs the band to play "Hail to the Chief."

Lincoln allows Rathbone and Harris to

Laura Keene as Portia, from the William Shakespeare play The Merchant of Venice.

The Ford's Theatre state box, restored to how it looked on the night of the assassination.
President Lincoln's rocking chair is on the left.

Ford's Theatre as seen from the stage.

enter the state box first, followed by Mary. Then he walks to the front of the box so the crowd can see him. The audience members rise to their feet and cheer, making a noise that Withers can only describe as "breathtaking." Lincoln bows twice as the audience cheers.

Only when the applause dies down does Lincoln ease into the rocking chair on the left side of the box.

⁕⁕⁕⁕⁕

A single door leads into the state box. On the other side of the door is a narrow, unlit hallway. At the end of the hallway is yet another door. This is the only route to and from the spot where Lincoln is sitting. It is John Parker's job to pull up a chair and wait in front of this hallway door, making sure that no one goes in or out.

But on the night of April 14, 1865, as Abraham Lincoln relaxes in his rocking chair and laughs out loud for the first time in months,

The rocking chair that was placed in the state box when President Lincoln was in the audience.

John Parker gets thirsty. He is bored, and he can't see the play. Taltavul's Star Saloon next door calls to him. Pushing his chair against the wall, he leaves the door to the state box hallway unguarded and walks outside. Charles Forbes is taking a nap on the driver's seat of Lincoln's carriage, oblivious to the fog and drizzle.

"How about a little ale?" Parker asks, knowing that Forbes will be an eager drinking buddy. The two walk into Taltavul's and make themselves comfortable. The show won't be over for two more hours—plenty of time to have a few beers before the Lincolns need them again.

Chapter 30

FRIDAY, APRIL 14, 1865
Washington, D. C.
9:30 P.M.

BOOTH GUIDES HIS HORSE into the alley behind Ford's Theatre. The night is quiet, except for the peals of laughter coming from inside the theater. He dismounts and shouts for Ned Spangler to come hold his horse. The stagehand appears at the back door, visibly distressed about the possibility of missing an all-important stage cue. Booth doesn't care. He demands that Spangler come outside and secure the animal. The last thing Booth needs is for his escape to be ruined by a runaway horse.

Spangler insists that he can't do the job. Booth persists. Spangler says he is willing to do anything for a great actor such as Booth—anything but lose his job. He dashes back into the theater and returns with Joseph Burroughs, a young boy who does odd jobs at Ford's Theatre and goes by the nickname "Peanut John." Booth hands Peanut John the reins and tells him to stay at the back door with the horse until he returns.

Peanut John, hoping that Booth will give him money for the

In the weeks following Lincoln's assassination, artists drew many imaginary scenes of the event. Here the artist John L. Magee shows Satan encouraging Booth to kill the president.

effort, agrees. He sits on the stone step and shivers in the damp night air, his fist clutched tightly around the reins.

Booth slides into the theater. The sound of the onstage actors speaking their lines fills the darkened backstage area. As he removes his riding gloves, he makes a show of saying hello to the cast and crew, most of whom he knows well. His eyes scrutinize the layout, memorizing the location of every stagehand and prop, not wanting anything to get in the way of his exit.

There is a tunnel under the stage, crossing from one side to the other. Booth checks to make sure that nothing clutters the passage. When he reaches the far side, Booth exits Ford's through yet another backstage door. This one leads to an alley, which runs down to Tenth Street. There's no one there.

Ford's Theatre is flanked on either side by taverns—the Green-back Saloon to the left and Taltavul's Star Saloon to the right. Theatergoers often go to one or the other for a drink at inter-mission. Now, feeling very pleased with himself, Booth pops into Taltavul's for a whiskey. He orders a whole bottle, then sits down at the bar. Incredibly, Lincoln's bodyguard is sipping a large tankard of ale just a few feet away.

At ten o'clock, Booth finally lowers his glass and walks back to Ford's Theatre.

1. Door that Booth shot from.
2. Chair the President sat in.
3. Where Booth jumped from.
4. Major Rathbone's seat.

From original painting of the inside of the box at Ford's Theatre, in which the President, Abraham Lincoln, was shot, on the night of April 14, 1865.

Painted by CHAS. GULAGER.

A painting of the inside of the state box at Ford's Theatre.

Chapter
31

FRIDAY, APRIL 14, 1865
Washington, D. C.
10:00 P.M.

THE THIRD ACT IS UNDER WAY. Soon the play will be over, and the Lincolns will return to the White House.

It is seven minutes past ten. After exchanging some small talk with ticket taker John Buckingham, who lets the actor in "courtesy of the house," Booth walks off. Buckingham's coworker Joseph Sessford points out that Booth has been in and out of the theater all day. "Wonder what he's up to?" Sessford mutters to Buckingham. They watch as Booth climbs the staircase to the dress circle, which leads to the hallway to the state box. But neither man thinks Booth's unusual behavior deserves closer scrutiny. They watch him disappear up the stairs and then return their attention to the front door and to the patrons returning late from intermission.

At the top of the stairs, Booth enters the dress circle lobby. He is now inside the darkened theater, standing directly behind the seats of the second-level audience.

Booth approaches the door leading into the state box hallway.

Ford's Theatre as seen from the left side of the audience section. The flag-draped state box is on the upper level. The doorway Booth used to access the state box hallway is to the right of the state box.

An illustration of the hallway leading to the state box.

He sees Charles Forbes sitting in John Parker's chair. Instead of staying in the tavern with Parker, the slightly drunk Forbes decided to go into the theater and sit in Parker's chair. Sensing that Forbes is not a regular guard, Booth manages to smooth talk the unsuspecting Forbes and gives him a piece of paper with some writing on it. Even though Forbes was questioned later by police about the meeting and the paper, the paper was never found and its message never revealed. Flattered by the attention of the famous actor, Forbes lets Booth step through the doorway without questioning him.

Booth now jams the wooden music stand he had seen earlier into the side of the door so that it wedges the door shut from the inside.

He creeps down the hallway. To get a better view of the president, he looks through the peephole in the wall at the back of the box. Authorities will later claim that Booth had carved the hole earlier in the day, but there is no proof of that.

Booth sees that Clara Harris and Major Rathbone are sitting along the wall to his far right, at an angle to the stage, and the Lincolns are along the railing.

He can hear the players down below, and he knows that, in a few short lines, Harry Hawk's character Asa Trenchard will be alone, delivering his "sockdologizing old man-trap" line.

Booth's cue is just ten seconds away.

He presses his black hat back down onto his head, then removes the derringer from his coat pocket and grasps it in his right fist. With his left hand, he slides the long, razor-sharp knife from its sheath.

Booth takes a deep breath and softly pushes the door open with his knife hand. The box is dimly lit from the footlights down below. He presses his body against the wall, careful to stay in the shadows while awaiting his cue. Abraham Lincoln's head is visible over the top of his rocking chair, just four short feet in front of Booth; then Lincoln looks down and to the left, at the audience.

"You sockdologizing old man-trap" booms out through the theater.

The audience explodes in laughter.

John Wilkes Booth
in typical expensive attire.

Chapter 32

FRIDAY, APRIL 14, 1865
Washington, D. C.
10:15 P.M.

A FEW BLOCKS AWAY, someone knocks hard on the front door of the "Old Clubhouse," the home of Secretary of State William Seward. The three-story brick house facing Lafayette Park, across the street from the White House, took that name from the time when it served as a boardinghouse and gathering place for congressmen.

There is another sharp knock, even though it's been only a few seconds since the first one. This time the pounding is more insistent. William Bell, a young black servant in a pressed white coat, hurries to the entryway.

"Yes, sir?" he asks, opening the door and seeing an unfamiliar face.

A handsome young man with long, thick hair stares back from the porch. He wears an expensive slouch hat and stands a few inches over six feet tall. His jaw is misshapen on the left, as if it was badly broken and then healed improperly. "I have medicine from Dr. Verdi," he says, holding up a small vial.

Secretary of State William Seward's home, known as the "Old Clubhouse."

"Yes, sir. I'll take it to him," Bell says, reaching for the bottle.

"It has to be delivered personally."

Bell looks at him curiously. Secretary Seward's physician had visited just an hour ago. Before leaving, he'd administered a sedative and insisted that there be no more visitors tonight. "Sir, I can't let you go upstairs. I have strict orders—"

"You're talking to a white man, boy. This medicine is for your master."

When Bell protests further, Lewis Powell pushes past him, saying, "I'm going up." Powell starts climbing the stairs. Bell is a

Lewis Powell after his capture, under guard at the Washington Navy Yard.

step behind at all times, pleading forgiveness and politely asking that Powell tread more softly so as not to wake the residents. "I'm sorry I talked rough to you," Bell says sheepishly.

"That's all right." Powell sighs, pleased that the hardest part of the plot is behind him. The next step is locating Seward's bedroom.

Suddenly the secretary's son Frederick stands at the top of the stairs, blocking Powell's path. He had been in bed, but the sound of Powell's boots pounding on the steps woke him. Young Seward demands to know Powell's business.

Politely, Powell holds up the medicine vial and swears that Dr. Verdi told him to deliver it to William Seward and William Seward only.

Frederick takes one look at Powell and misjudges him as a simpleton. Rather than argue, he walks into his father's bedroom to see if he is awake.

This is the break the assassin is looking for.

Frederick Seward returns. "He's sleeping. Give it to me."

"I was ordered to give it to the secretary."

"You cannot see Mr. Seward. I am his son and the assistant secretary of state. Go back and tell the doctor that I refused to let you go into the sickroom because Mr. Seward was sleeping."

"Very well, sir," says Powell, handing Frederick the vial. "I will go."

After Frederick Seward accepts the vial, Powell takes three steps down the stairs. Suddenly he turns. He sprints back up to the landing, drawing his revolver. He levels the pistol, curses, and pulls the trigger.

Frederick cries out in fear, throwing up his arms to defend himself. He will later tell police he thought he was a dead man. But the pistol jams. The two men struggle until Powell leaps up onto the landing and hits Frederick with the butt of his revolver, knocking him unconscious.

Lewis Powell continues to pound on Frederick's head without mercy, blood spattering the walls and his

An illustration showing Frederick Seward fighting for his life against Lewis Powell.

David Herold.

own hands and face. The beating is so savage that the pistol literally falls to pieces in his hands. Only then does he stand up straight and begin walking toward the secretary of state's bedroom.

"Murder, murder, murder!" William Bell cries from the ground floor. He sprints out the front door, screaming at the top of his lungs.

Across the street, in the shadow of a tree, David Herold holds the two getaway horses. Bell's cries are sure to bring soldiers and police. Herold panics. He ties Powell's horse to a tree, mounts his own horse, and gallops down Fifteenth Street.

Chapter
33

FRIDAY, APRIL 14, 1865
Washington, D. C.
10:15 P.M.

THE COMMOTION IN THE HALLWAY has alerted twenty-year-old Fanny Seward. The daughter of the secretary of state has been sitting at the foot of her father's bed. Also inside the room is Sergeant George Robinson. Now Robinson leans his full weight against the door as the assassin tries to push his way in. But Lewis Powell forces open the door and slashes at Robinson with his knife, cutting the soldier's forehead to the bone and almost putting out an eye. As Robinson crumples to the ground, Fanny Seward places herself between Powell and her father. "Please don't kill him," she begs, terrified.

Powell punches Fanny Seward in the face, knocking her unconscious. A split second later, he is on the bed, plunging his knife into Seward's neck and shoulders.

The room is pitch-black, except for the sliver of light from the open door. Powell's first thrust misses, making a hollow thud as it slams into the headboard.

Powell kneels over Seward, stabbing him again and again and again. The secretary wears a splint on his broken jaw, which, luckily, deflects the knife away from the jugular vein, but it does little to protect the rest of his skull. The right side of his face is sliced away from the bone and now hangs like a flap.

The assassin is almost finished. Powell brings up his knife for one final blow. But at that moment, Seward's son Augustus, a career

An illustration of the fight with the assassin in William Seward's room.

army officer, enters the room. Powell leaps at Seward, stabbing him seven times. In the midst of the attack, Robinson staggers to his feet and rejoins the fight. Robinson is stabbed four more times. Powell then races from the room, still clutching his knife.

At that very moment, State Department messenger Emerick Hansell arrives at the door on official business. He sees Powell, covered with blood, running down the steps. Powell stabs the messenger.

"I'm mad! I'm mad!" Powell screams as he runs into the night, hoping to scare off anyone who might try to stop him.

Upon exiting the house, Powell throws the blood-covered knife into the gutter. He then looks for David Herold and their getaway horses. Seeing nothing, he listens for the telltale clip-clop of approaching horseshoes.

"Murder! Murder!" William Bell cries from the porch. Soldiers who have been stationed nearby on guard duty in the neighborhood come running. Powell sees his horse now, tied to the tree where Herold left it, and his heart sinks. He knows that without Herold he will be lost on the streets of Washington. Still, he can't very well just stand around. Powell unties the horse and mounts. He has the good sense to wipe the blood and sweat from his face with a handkerchief. Then, instead of galloping away, he nudges his heels gently into the horse's flanks and trots casually down Fifteenth Street, with William Bell running behind him, shouting "Murder!" But instead of stopping him, the unsuspecting soldiers ignore the black man and run right past Powell.

After a block and a half, Bell falls behind. He eventually returns to the Seward home, where four gravely injured men and one woman lie. Miraculously, they will all recover.

Lewis Powell trots his horse toward the edge of town. He hides in a field and wonders if he will ever find a way out of Washington.

George Atzerodt's two Bowie knives.
Bowie knives came in a variety of sizes and styles.
They were noted for having long blades,
some up to twenty-four inches long.

Chapter
34

FRIDAY, APRIL 14, 1865
Washington, D. C.
10:15 P.M.

GEORGE ATZERODT is drinking hard. Like his target, Andrew Johnson, Atzerodt is staying at Kirkwood House, on the corner of Pennsylvania Avenue and Twelfth Street, four blocks from the White House and just one block from Ford's Theatre.

At nine thirty, Atzerodt visits J. Naylor's stable on E Street to pick up his horse. The stable manager, John Fletcher, knows Atzerodt and his friend David Herold and does not care for either of them. Nevertheless, when a nervous, sweating Atzerodt asks if he'd like to get a drink, Fletcher answers with a quick "don't mind if I do." He is concerned about Herold, who rented a horse from him earlier that day and is long overdue. Fletcher hopes that Atzerodt will disclose his friend's location after a drink or two.

They walk to the bar at the Union Hotel. Atzerodt, who Fletcher suspects has been drinking for some time, orders a whiskey; Fletcher asks for a tankard of ale. After just one drink, Atzerodt pays, and they return to the stable, with Fletcher none the wiser about Herold's location.

"Your friend is staying out very late with his horse," Fletcher finally prods. Atzerodt has just handed him a five-dollar tip for boarding his horse.

"He'll be back after a while," Atzerodt replies as he mounts the mare and returns to Kirkwood House.

Andrew Johnson, meanwhile, eats an early dinner alone. Largely

A typical livery stable in Washington, D.C., in 1865.

uneducated, he learned to read and write late in his life. He was a tailor by trade and entered politics in his twenties, working his way up to the Senate. He owes a lot to President Lincoln, who first appointed him the military governor of Tennessee and then chose him to run on the vice presidential ticket after Lincoln asked Hannibal Hamlin of Maine to step down. Hamlin was a Northerner, and Lincoln needed a Southern presence on the ticket.

At ten fifteen, George Atzerodt is at the bar in Kirkwood House, getting drunk. Truth be told, he wants no part of murder. A few floors above him, Johnson lies alone in his room. In his lifetime, he will suffer the public shame of impeachment. Andrew Johnson will not, however, suffer the far worse fate of death at the hand of an assassin. For that, Johnson can thank the effects of alcohol, as a now very drunk George Atzerodt continues to raise his glass.

An election medal showing Andrew Johnson.

FRIDAY, APRIL 14, 1865
Washington, D. C.
10:15 P.M.

J OHN WILKES BOOTH TAKES A BOLD STEP out of the shadows, derringer clutched in his right fist and knife in his left. He extends his arm and aims for the back of Abraham Lincoln's head.

Booth squeezes the trigger.

* * *

Dr. Joseph Janvier Woodward's autopsy report, written at noon on April 15 and smeared with Lincoln's blood, will read, "The ball had entered through the occipital bone about one inch to the left of the median line and just above the left lateral sinus, which it opened. It then penetrated the dura mater, passed through the posterior lobe of the cerebrum, entered the left lateral ventricle and lodged in the white matter of the cerebrum just above the anterior portion of the left corpus striatum."

During the autopsy, the president's calvarium—or skullcap—will be removed with a saw. A surgeon will probe the exposed

*A lithograph by an unknown artist showing John Wilkes Booth
shooting President Abraham Lincoln.*

brain before slicing into it with a scalpel, using the path of coagu-
lated blood to trace the path of the ball. This will show that it
entered behind Lincoln's left ear and traveled diagonally across the
brain, coming to rest above his right eye.

———◆•✕•◆———

At the instant of being shot, President Abraham Lincoln slumps
forward in his rocking chair. Mary Lincoln, lost in the play until
this very moment, stops laughing. Major Rathbone snaps his head
around at the sound of gunfire. He is on his feet immediately.

John Wilkes Booth drops the derringer and switches the knife to his right hand. Major Rathbone vaults across the small space. Booth raises the knife and brings it down in a hacking motion. Rathbone throws his left arm up in a defensive reflex and feels the knife cut him to the bone.

Booth moves quickly. He steps to the front of the box. "Freedom!" he bellows down to the audience.

Booth hurls his body over the railing. But he briefly gets caught in the portrait of President Washington and misjudges the thickness of the bunting decorating the front of the box. Booth's right spur tangles in the folds of the cloth. Instead of a gallant two-footed landing on the stage, Booth topples heavily from the state box and lands awkwardly.

The fibula of Booth's lower left leg, a thin bone that is not intended to bear weight, snaps just above his ankle. The fracture is complete, dividing the bone into two neat pieces. If not for the tightness of Booth's boot, which forms an immediate splint, the bone would be poking through the skin.

James Ford steps out of the box office thinking Booth is pulling some crazy stunt to get attention. Observers in the audience have heard the pop and are amazed by the famous actor making a sudden surprise appearance on the stage—perhaps adding some comical whimsy to this very special evening. Harry Hawk still stands center stage, his head turned toward Booth, wondering why in the world he would intrude on the performance.

Then the assassin takes charge and shouts, as he had planned, "*Sic semper tyrannis!*"

An illustration showing John Wilkes Booth on the stage of Ford's Theatre immediately after he shot the president. Mary Lincoln and Lincoln's slumped body are in the upper middle.

The rocking chair President Abraham Lincoln was sitting in when he was shot.

Booth limps off the stage "with a motion," observes one spectator, "like the hopping of a bull frog."

"Stop that man!" Major Rathbone screams from above.

"Won't somebody please stop that man!" Clara Harris echoes.

"What is the matter?" cries a voice from the audience.

"The president has been shot!" Clara shouts back.

The theater explodes in confusion. Men climb up and over the seats, some fleeing toward the exits while others race to the stage. Women faint.

Meanwhile, Booth passes within inches of leading lady Laura Keene as he limps off the stage. William Withers, the orchestra leader, stands between Booth and the stage door. Withers is paralyzed with fear, but Booth assumes he is intentionally blocking the way and slashes at him, "the sharp blade ripping through the collar of my coat, penetrating my vest and under garments, and inflicting a flesh wound in my neck," Withers will later testify.

Only one man is bold enough to give chase. Set carpenter Jake Ritterspaugh and Booth reach the stage door at the same time. Booth thrusts the knife blade at him. Ritterspaugh leaps back. And in that instant, Booth is gone, squeezing through the door and hauling himself up into the saddle.

Rather than give Peanut John the nickel the boy had hoped for, Booth kicks him hard and hits him with the butt of his knife.

"He kicked me! He kicked me!" the boy moans, falling to the ground.

At the same instant, a spontaneous torchlight parade blocks Booth's getaway on Tenth Street. He swerves into the alley, spurs his horse down the cobblestones between two large brick buildings, and turns onto F Street, avoiding the procession.

John Wilkes Booth disappears into the night.

One of John Wilkes Booth's spurs.

Chapter 36

FRIDAY, APRIL 14, 1865
Washington, D. C.
10:20 P.M.

WORD IS ALREADY SPREADING through Washington that the president has been shot. People aren't racing away from Ford's, they're racing *to* Ford's to see for themselves if these wild rumors are true.

Now a troop of cavalry arrives and plunges recklessly through the crowd assembling outside the theater. Inside, the audience surges toward the stage, chanting all the while that Booth must be caught and killed immediately. Laura Keene has the presence of mind to march to center stage and cry out for calm and sanity, but her words go unheeded.

Soon more bad news begins to spread: Secretary Seward has been assaulted in his bed.

In front of the Willard Hotel, John Fletcher is still seething that David Herold hasn't returned the horse he rented earlier. At that very moment, Herold trots past. "You get off that horse now!" Fletcher cries, springing out into the street and reaching for the

A drawing by Thomas Nast of the gentleman's reading parlor in the Willard Hotel. Typically men would meet in hotel parlors like this to conduct business and discuss issues of the day.

bridle. But Herold spurs the horse and gallops away. Acting quickly, Fletcher sprints back to his stable, saddles a horse for himself, and races after him.

Meanwhile, Booth proceeds unchallenged through the streets. There are plenty of men riding horses through town. It's only when he finally nears the end of his three-mile journey to the Navy Yard Bridge that his fears about being caught force him to spur the horse and ride hard to freedom.

It is ten forty-five when Booth pulls back on the reins once again and canters up to the wooden drawbridge by the Navy Yard. Booth approaches like a man confident that his path will go unblocked. "Where are you going, sir?" cries the military sentry. His name is Silas T. Cobb, and his long and boring shift will be over at midnight. He notices the lather on the horse's flanks, a sign that it's been ridden hard.

"Home. Down in Charles," Booth replies.

"Didn't you know, my friend, that it is against the laws to pass here after nine o'clock?" When the war started in 1861, a curfew was established around the capital and strictly enforced. Cobb is required to challenge anyone entering or exiting Washington, but the truth is that, since the war is almost over, the formal restrictions on crossing the bridge after curfew have ended. He wants no trouble, just to finish his shift in peace and get a good night's sleep.

"No," lies Booth. He explains that he's been waiting for the full moon to rise so that he might navigate the darkened roads by night.

"I will pass you," Cobb sighs. "But I don't know I ought to."

Major Rathbone's gloves worn on the night of President Lincoln's assassination.

"Hell, I guess there'll be no trouble about that," Booth shoots back.

Booth is barely across the Potomac when David Herold approaches the bridge. He gives his name as just Smith. Once again, after a brief discussion, Cobb lets him pass.

One more rider approaches Cobb that night. He is John Fletcher. Fletcher can clearly see Herold on the other side of the bridge, disappearing into the Maryland night.

"You can cross," Cobb tells him, "but my orders say I can't let anyone back across the bridge until morning."

The Maryland countryside, with its smugglers and spies and bandits, is the last place Fletcher wants to spend the night. He turns his horse back toward the stable.

A wooden drawbridge in 1865, similar to the one by the Navy Yard.

Chapter
37

FRIDAY, APRIL 14, 1865
Washington, D. C.
10:20 P.M.

L INCOLN'S LIFE IS SLIPPING AWAY. Mary Lincoln lays her head on the president's chest as Major Rathbone uses his one good arm to yank away the music stand blocking the door.

The major swings open the outer door of the state box. Dozens of unruly theatergoers try to barge in. "Doctors only!" Rathbone shouts as blood drips down his arm and pools on the floor.

"I'm bleeding to death!" Rathbone says as a twenty-three-year-old doctor, Charles Leale, fights his way forward. Dr. Leale came to the theater because he wanted to see Lincoln in person. Now he is the first physician to come upon the crime scene. Leale gives Rathbone a quick physical examination. Noting that Rathbone is not bleeding to death, Dr. Leale turns his attention to Lincoln.

"Oh, Doctor," sobs Mary Lincoln as Leale slowly removes her from her husband's body. "Can he recover? Will you take charge of him?"

"I will do what I can," Dr. Leale says calmly. With a nod to the crowd of men who have followed him into the box, the young doctor makes it clear that Mary must be moved. She is ushered to a couch on the other side of the box, next to Clara Harris, who begins stroking her hand.

Leale orders that no one else be admitted to the state box except for physicians. Then he stands in front of the rocking chair, facing Lincoln's slumped head. He pushes Lincoln's body upright, and his head lolls back against the rocker. Leale can feel a slight breath from Lincoln's nose and mouth, but he is reluctant to move the body without making a preliminary examination. One thing, however, is clear: Lincoln is not dead.

Dr. Leale can't see the injury. Onlookers light matches for him, and the call goes out for a lamp. The front of Lincoln's body shows no sign of physical violence, and the forward slumping indicates that the attack must have come from behind.

Dr. Charles A. Leale.

A fanciful depiction of the bullet used to assassinate President Lincoln.

Yet there's no visible entry wound or exit wound. If Dr. Leale didn't know better, he would swear that Lincoln simply dozed off and will awaken any minute.

"Put him on the floor," the doctor orders. Gently, Lincoln's long torso is lifted by men standing on both sides of the rocking chair and then lowered to the carpet.

Because he saw that Major Rathbone's wounds were caused by a knife, and because he hadn't heard any gunshots during the performance, Leale deduces that Lincoln was stabbed. He rolls the president on one side and carefully searches for a puncture wound, his fingers slipping along the skin, probing for a telltale oozing of blood. But he feels nothing, and when he pulls his hands away, they're clean.

He strips Lincoln to the waist and continues the search, cutting off the president's white shirt with a pocketknife. But his skin is smooth, with no sign of any harm. Leale lifts Lincoln's eyelids and examines the pupils. He waves his hand back and forth. The pupils do not respond. He decides to reexamine Lincoln's head. Perhaps he was stabbed in the back of his skull.

Dr. Leale runs his hands through Lincoln's hair. This time they come back red with blood.

Alarmed, Leale examines the president's head a second time.

Beneath the thick hair, just above and behind the left ear, hides a small blood clot. It's no bigger than the doctor's pinkie finger, but when he pulls his finger away, the result is like a cork being removed from a bottle. Blood flows freely from the wound, and reflexively Lincoln's chest suddenly rises and falls as pressure is taken from his brain.

Dr. Leale knows just what to do—and he does it well.

Working quickly, he straddles Lincoln's chest and begins resuscitating the president, hoping to improve the flow of oxygen to his brain. He shoves two fingers down Lincoln's throat and presses down on the back of the tongue, just in case food or drink is lodged in the esophagus. As he does so, two other doctors who were in the audience arrive on the scene. Though they are far more experienced, army surgeon Dr. Charles Sabin Taft and Dr. Albert King defer to their younger colleague because Dr. Leale was first on the scene. When he asks them to stimulate the blood flow by manipulating Lincoln's arms in an up-and-down, back-and-forth manner, each instantly kneels and takes an arm. Leale, meanwhile, presses hard on Lincoln's torso, trying to stimulate his heart.

Then, as Leale will one day tell an audience celebrating the one hundredth anniversary of Lincoln's birth, he performs an act of great and urgent intimacy: "I leaned forcibly forward directly over his body, thorax to thorax, face to face, and several times drew in a long breath, then forcibly breathed directly into his mouth and nostrils, which expanded the lungs and improved his respirations."

Every bit of his energy is poured into accomplishing the task of saving Lincoln. Finally, Dr. Leale knows in his heart that the

The state box where Dr. Leale examined President Lincoln.

procedure has not worked. He will later recall, "After waiting a moment I placed my ear over his thorax and found the action of the heart improving. I arose to the erect kneeling posture, then watched for a short time, and saw that the President could continue independent breathing and that instant death would not occur. I then pronounced my diagnosis and prognosis."

But Dr. Leale does not utter the hopeful words the onlookers wish to hear.

Dr. Leale has seen Lincoln's pupils. The pupil of the left eye is severely contracted, and the pupil of the right eye is widely dilated. Neither responds to changes in the light, a sure sign that his brain has been severely damaged. "His wound is mortal," Leale announces softly. "It is impossible for him to recover."

❦

A soldier vomits. Men remove their caps. Mary Lincoln sits just a few feet away but is in too much shock to understand what's been said. Someone hands Dr. Leale a glass of brandy and water, which he slowly dribbles into Lincoln's mouth. Though the president's brain is dead, his body remains alive and is able to function at a survival level. Lincoln's prominent Adam's apple bobs as he swallows.

The uproar in the theater, meanwhile, has not diminished. No one in the state box speaks as Dr. Leale works on Lincoln, but its list of occupants grows longer. With John Parker, Lincoln's bodyguard, still missing, no one is blocking access to the little room. On the couch,

The coat President Lincoln was wearing the night he was assassinated.

the distraught Mary Lincoln is being comforted by Clara Harris. Major Rathbone drips blood on the carpet, trying to stanch the flow by holding tight to his injured arm. Three doctors, a half dozen soldiers, and a small number of theater patrons have battled their way into the box. And then the actress Laura Keene forces her way into their midst and kneels at Lincoln's side. She begs to be allowed to rest Lincoln's head on her lap. Dr. Leale, somewhat stunned but knowing it can do no harm, agrees.

Keene lifts the president's head into her lap and calmly strokes his face. The chestnut-eyed actress with long auburn hair knows that this moment will put her name in papers around the world, so there is more than a touch of self-indulgence in her actions. But like everyone else in the state box, she is stunned. Just a few minutes

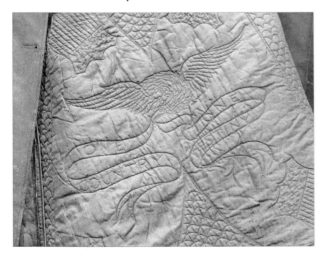

before, the president of the United States had been a vibrant and larger-than-life presence. Now everything has changed.

Detail of the lining of President Lincoln's coat. Note the phrase "One country, one destiny."

Chapter 38

FRIDAY, APRIL 14, 1865
Washington, D.C.
11 P.M.

THE PRESIDENT OF THE UNITED STATES cannot die on a dirty floor. No one knows how much longer he will live, but he must be moved. Dr. King suggests they move him to the White House, where he can pass the final moments of life in the comfort of his own bed. But Dr. Leale knows better than to attempt a bumpy carriage ride through the crowded city streets. "He will be dead before we get there," Leale says firmly.

The young doctor agrees, however, that Lincoln should be resting in a bed, not on the floor. Dr. Taft sends a soldier to search nearby boardinghouses for an empty room. He orders four other young soldiers to lift Lincoln back into the rocking chair and carry the president out of the theater.

But Dr. Leale overrules Taft. A stretcher would be ideal, but none is available. Leale orders the four soldiers to get to work, lock their hands beneath the president, and form a sling. Two will lift his torso, while two will carry his legs. They will transport Lincoln headfirst. Leale will walk backward, cradling Lincoln's head in his hands.

Laura Keene steps aside as the four soldiers of the Pennsylvania Light Artillery—John Corey, Jabes Griffiths, Bill Sample, and Jacob Soles—slip their hands under that torso and raise Lincoln to a sitting position. Dr. Leale, with help from the other two physicians, buttons the president's coat.

"Guards," barks Leale, "clear the passage."

Through the hallway, out into the dress circle, and down the stairs they travel. Mary Lincoln follows behind, stunned and shaky.

"Clear the way," Leale orders. Soldiers in the crowd push back the mob. They finally reach the lobby but don't know where to go next. By now, soldiers have found a partition usually used to divide the state box. At seven feet long and three inches thick, it makes a perfect stretcher for Abraham Lincoln. His body is shifted onto the board.

Dr. Leale and the two other surgeons decide they will carry Lincoln into Taltavul's, right next door. A soldier is sent to clear the tavern. But he soon comes back with word that Lincoln will not be allowed inside. Peter Taltavul is a patriot, a man who spent twenty-five years in the Marine Corps band. He is one of the few who has the foresight to understand the significance of how the night's events will one day be viewed. "Don't bring him in here," Taltavul tells the soldier. "It shouldn't be said that the president of the United States died in a saloon."

Leale orders that Lincoln be lifted and carried to the row houses

A painting by an unknown artist of the scene of President Lincoln being carried out of Ford's Theatre.

across the street. There is an enormous crowd in front of Ford's. It will be almost impossible to clear a path through their midst, but it's vital that Leale get Lincoln someplace warm and clean, immediately. The makeshift stretcher is lifted, and Lincoln's body is carried out into the cold, wet night.

Then Lincoln's bodyguards arrive. Not John Parker—the instant he heard that Lincoln was shot, he vanished into the night. No, it is the Union Light Guard, otherwise known as the Seventh Independent Company of Ohio Volunteer Cavalry, that gallops to the rescue. They raced over from their stables next to the White House when they heard about the shooting. Rather than dismount, they work with other soldiers on the scene to make a corridor from one side of Tenth Street to the other. Leale and the men carrying Lincoln make their way down Ford's granite front steps and onto the muddy road, still not knowing where they are going.

"Bring him in here," a voice shouts above the madness.

Henry S. Safford is a twenty-five-year-old War Department employee. He has toasted the Union victory every night since Monday, and tonight he felt so worn out that he stayed in his rented room in William Petersen's boardinghouse to rest. He was alone in his parlor, reading, when the streets below him exploded in confusion. When Safford stuck his head out the window to see what was happening, someone shouted the news that Lincoln had been shot. Safford raced downstairs and out into the crowd, but "finding it impossible to go further, as everyone acted crazy or mad," he retreated. Safford stood on the porch and watched in amazement as Lincoln's body was carried out of Ford's. He saw Leale lift his head, scanning the street, searching for someplace to bring Lincoln.

Now Safford wants to help.

"Put him in here," he shouts again.

Dr. Leale was actually aiming for the house next door, but a soldier had tried and found it locked. So they turn toward Safford.

Leale and his stretcher bearers carry Lincoln up nine short, curved steps to the front door. "Take us to your best room," he orders Safford. And though he is hardly the man to be making that decision, Safford realizes that his own

A late-twentieth-century photograph of the Petersen House, where Lincoln was carried.

second-floor room will not do. He guides the group down to the spacious room of George and Huldah Francis, but it is locked. Safford leads them to another room. He pushes open the door and sees that it is empty. It is clearly not Petersen's finest—but it will have to do.

The room is rented to William Clark, a twenty-three-year-old army clerk who is gone for the night. At just under ten feet wide and eighteen feet long, the room is furnished with a four-poster bed, a table, a bureau, and chairs. It is a cramped but very clean and neat space.

Lincoln is much too big for the bed. Dr. Leale orders that the headboard be broken off, but it won't break. Instead, the president is laid down diagonally on the red, white, and blue bedspread. His head points toward the door and his feet toward the wall. Ironically, John Wilkes Booth had often rented this very room during the previous summer.

The room where Lincoln died. The Petersen House is now a national historical site, and the building and rooms are preserved and restored to the setting of President Lincoln's final hours.

Everyone leaves but the doctors and Mary Lincoln. She stares down at her husband; there are two pillows under his head, and his bearded chin rests on his chest. Now and then, he sighs involuntarily, giving her hope.

"Mrs. Lincoln, I must ask you to leave," Dr. Leale says softly.

Mary is like a child, so forlorn that she lacks the will to protest as others make decisions for her. The first lady steps out of William Clark's room, into the long, dark hallway.

"Live," she pleads to her husband before she leaves. "You must live."

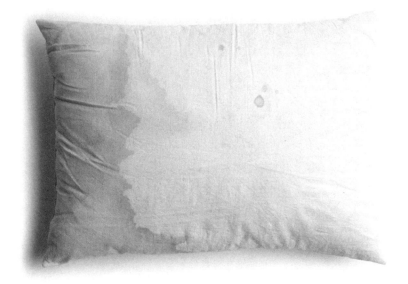

The pillow on which Abraham Lincoln's head rested showing bloodstains.

Chapter
39

SATURDAY, APRIL 15, 1865
Washington, D. C.
Midnight

DR. LEALE STRIPS LINCOLN'S BODY. He searches it for signs of other wounds but finds none.

Examining the long, slender body, Leale is disturbed to feel that Lincoln's feet are now icy to the touch. The doctor tells a soldier in the room what he needs and orders the soldier to obtain the items at the Lincoln General Hospital, a nearby military facility. Soldiers soon arrive from the hospital with hot water, brandy, blankets, and materials to make a mustard plaster. Dr. Leale immediately applies a mustard plaster to every inch of the front of Lincoln's body, from shoulders down to ankles. "No drug or medicine in any form was administered to the president," he will later note. "But the artificial heat and mustard plaster that I had applied warmed his cold body and stimulated his nerves."

He then covers the president with a blanket as Dr. Taft begins the process of removing the bullet from Lincoln's head. Taft inserts his index finger into the wound and pronounces that it has penetrated beyond the length of his fingertip.

More brandy and water is poured between Lincoln's lips. His Adam's apple once again bobs during the first spoonful but not at all for the second. With great difficulty, the doctors gently turn Lincoln on his side so that the excess fluid will run from his mouth and not choke him.

The doctors can do nothing for the president but monitor his vital signs. The deathwatch has begun. A normal man would have been dead by now.

Dr. Leale sends messengers out to find Robert Lincoln and bring him before his father dies. Messages also go out to Surgeon General Joseph K. Barnes and a few other doctors, including Lincoln's family physician, Dr. Robert King Stone, as well as the president's pastor, the Reverend Dr. Phineas D. Gurley.

Dr. Barnes arrives and takes control of the scene. He is closely followed by the future surgeon general Charles H. Crane. Dr. Leale explains his course of action in great detail to these two powerful

Surgeon General Joseph K. Barnes.

and well-regarded physicians. Both men agree with Leale's decisions and treatment, much to the young physician's relief.

Dr. Leale realizes that he is no longer needed in that cramped bedroom. But he does not leave. Leale, like the others, can barely hold back his tears. He has noticed that Lincoln is visibly more comfortable when the wound is unclogged. So he sits next to the dying man's head, poking his finger into the blood clot every few minutes, making sure there's not too much pressure on Lincoln's brain.

Outside, the crowd waits to hear the latest news. Even when a light rain starts falling, they will not leave. Secretary of War Stanton arrives, makes the room next to Lincoln's his headquarters, and takes charge, acting as interim president of the United States.

Word of the assassination has brought a number of government officials to the Petersen House. The police investigation is beginning to take shape. It is clear that Booth shot Lincoln, and many believe that the actor also attacked Seward in his bed. Vice President Andrew Johnson, whose luck held when his assassin backed out, now stands in the next room, summoned there after learning of Lincoln's condition.

The occupants of the bedroom change constantly, with clergymen, government officials, and other people stepping in for a moment to pay their respects. More than sixty-five people will be allowed inside before the night is through. The most frequent presence is Mary Lincoln, who weeps and even falls to her knees by the bed when she is allowed a few moments with her husband. Leale

takes care to spread a clean white handkerchief over the bloody pillow whenever
she is about to walk in, but the bleeding
from Lincoln's head never ceases, and before
Mary Lincoln departs, the handkerchief is
often covered in blood and brain matter.

At three A.M., the scene is so horrible that
Mary is no longer admitted.

The various doctors take turns recording
Lincoln's condition. His breathing is shallow
and fast, coming twenty-four to twenty-seven
times a minute. His pulse rises to sixty-four at
five forty A.M. and hovers at sixty just a few
moments later. By that time, Leale can barely
feel it.

One of the physicians in the room, Dr.
Ezra Abbott, makes notes on Lincoln's
condition:

> 6:30—still failing and labored breathing.
> 6:40—expirations prolonged and groaning.
> A deep, softly sonorous cooing sound at
> the end of each expiration, audible to
> bystanders.
> 6:45—respiration uneasy, choking and
> grunting. Lower jaw relaxed. Mouth open. A minute with-
> out a breath. Face getting dark.

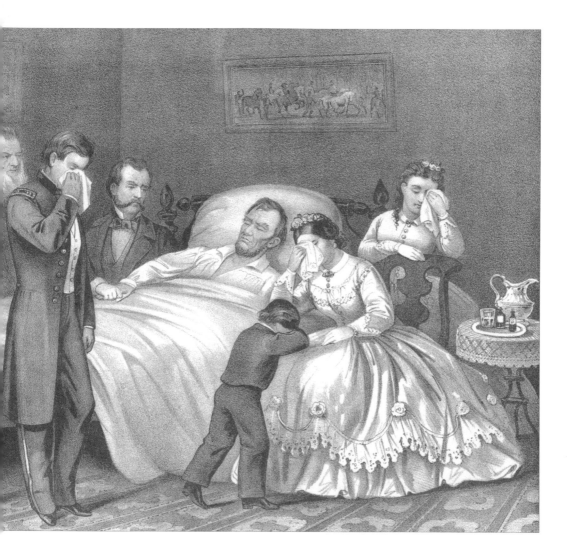

A Currier & Ives lithograph of the death of President Abraham Lincoln. This is a romanticized image. Lincoln's wife and son were not in the room when he died.

6:59—breathes again a little more at intervals.

7:00—still breathing at long pauses; symptoms of immediate dissolution.

With the president's death near, Mary Lincoln is once again admitted. Dr. Leale stands to make room. She sits in the chair next to Lincoln and then presses her face against her husband's. "Love," she says softly, "speak to me."

A "loud, unnatural noise," in Dr. Leale's description, barks up from Lincoln's lungs. The sound is so grotesque that Mary collapses. As she is carried from the room, she steals one last glimpse of her husband. She has known him since he was just a country lawyer and

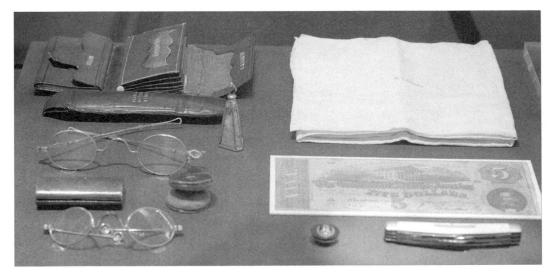

The contents of Lincoln's pockets on the night of his assassination.

A life mask casting of Abraham Lincoln's face and hands on display at Ford's Theatre. The face was made in 1860 just before Lincoln was nominated.

has shared almost half her life with him. This will be the last time she sees him alive.

"I have given my husband to die," she laments, wishing that it could have been her instead.

Dr. Leale can't find a pulse. Lincoln's breathing becomes harsh, then ceases altogether before starting again. The room fills with a small army of elected officials, all of whom wish to witness the historic moment of Lincoln's death. Outside, it is dawn, and the crowds have grown even larger.

In the bedroom, Robert Lincoln, who arrived a few minutes ago, sobs loudly, unable to control his grief. He stands at the head of the bed and looks down at his father. Dr. Barnes sits in the chair, his finger on Lincoln's carotid artery, seeking a pulse. Dr. Leale has moved to the other side of the bed and wedged himself against the wall. He once again holds Lincoln's hand, simultaneously using his index finger to feel for a pulse on Lincoln's wrist.

Lincoln draws his last breath at seven twenty-one. His heart beats regularly for another fifteen seconds, then stops altogether at ten seconds past seven twenty-two A.M.

More than twenty men are packed into the bedroom. Nobody says a word for five long minutes. Dr. Barnes reaches into his vest pocket for a pair of silver coins, which he places over Lincoln's eyes. Dr. Leale, meanwhile, folds the president's arms across his chest and carefully smooths his hair.

He barely hears Secretary Stanton's words: "Now he belongs to the ages."

PART FOUR

CHASING THE ASSASSINS

SATURDAY, APRIL 15, 1865
Maryland Countryside
Early Morning

JOHN WILKES BOOTH and David Herold have escaped into the Maryland countryside. They meet up at their rendezvous spot of Soper's Hill in the dead of night. There is no sign of Atzerodt or Powell, so Booth and Herold push on with their flight toward Virginia. However, Booth's leg injury is so severe, and their horses are so tired, that they have been forced to find a place to rest. They are now hiding in the house of the physician and Confederate sympathizer Dr. Samuel Mudd, whose farm is about twenty-five miles south of Washington.

In Washington, investigators stumble upon Atzerodt's trail first. After failing to carry out the assassination of Vice President Johnson, he spent the night wandering around Washington, getting thoroughly drunk in a number of bars and making sure to dispose of the knife that was supposed to be the murder weapon. Atzerodt is all too aware that returning to his room at Kirkwood House would be a stupid idea. So just before three A.M., he checks into the

Pennsylvania House Hotel, where he is assigned a double room. His roommate is a police lieutenant named W. R. Keim. The two men know each other from Atzerodt's previous stays at the Pennsylvania House. They lie on their backs in the darkness and have a short conversation before falling asleep. Keim is stunned by the slaying of Lincoln. As drunk as he is, Atzerodt does an artful job of pretending sadness, saying that the whole Lincoln assassination is a terrible tragedy.

Meanwhile, detectives are combing through his belongings at Kirkwood House. A desk clerk tells them he remembers seeing a "villainous-looking" individual registered in room 126. Atzerodt took the only room key with him when he fled, so detectives have to break down the door to investigate. Quickly canvassing the room, they come up with the first solid leads about Lincoln's murder. In the breast pocket of a dark coat hanging on a wall peg, they discover a ledger book from a bank in Montreal. The name written inside the cover is that of John Wilkes Booth, whom many eyewitnesses have identified as Lincoln's killer. The book confirms the connection between Atzerodt and Booth.

Dr. Samuel Mudd.

Searching through the bed, the detectives find a loaded revolver under the pillow and a knife underneath the covers. In fact, room 126 is a treasure trove of evidence: a map of Southern states, pistol rounds, a handkerchief embroidered with the name of Booth's mother, and much more.

Investigators now have two suspects: Booth and Atzerodt. Warrants are issued for their arrests.

At the same time, a tip leads investigators to raid Mary Surratt's boardinghouse on H Street. Nothing is found, but Surratt's behavior is suspicious enough that detectives decide to keep an eye on her and the house. A similar tip leads police to room 228 at the National Hotel—Booth's room—which is quickly ripped apart. Booth also has left behind clues—among them a business card bearing the name J. Harrison Surratt and a letter from Samuel Arnold, who had been part of the kidnapping plot, that implicates Michael O'Laughlen. It is obvious that John Wilkes Booth did not act alone.

A few blocks away, detectives question Secretary of State Seward's household staff and add two more nameless individuals to the list: the man who attacked Seward and his accomplice, who was seen waiting outside. This brings the number of conspirators to six: Booth, Atzerodt, O'Laughlen, Arnold, and Seward's two unknown attackers.

Meanwhile, Washington is in a state of shock. Flags are flown at half-mast. Vice President Andrew Johnson is sworn in as the seventeenth president of the United States.

Throughout the nation, as the news spreads, Abraham Lincoln's worst fears are being realized. Outraged Northerners mourn his loss and openly pledge revenge, while Southerners rejoice in the death of the man who wouldn't give them the freedom to form their own nation. The Civil War seems on the verge of erupting once again.

Believing that catching Lincoln's killer will end the unrest,

An illustration showing Andrew Johnson taking the oath of office for the presidency of the United States.

Secretary of War Stanton spends Saturday expanding the search, making the hunt for Lincoln's killers the biggest in American history. Soldiers, cavalry, and law enforcement officers throughout the Northern states are ordered to devote all their energies to finding John Wilkes Booth and his band of killers. Stanton sends a telegram to New York City, recalling Lafayette C. Baker, his former spymaster and chief of security, to help him in this effort.

As all this is going on, George Atzerodt wakes up at dawn on Saturday morning. He leaves the Pennsylvania House and walks across the city to nearby Georgetown, where he makes the unusual gesture of calling on Lucinda Metz, an old girlfriend. He tells her he is going away for a while, as if she might somehow want to come along. And then as mysteriously as he appears, Atzerodt leaves and pawns his revolver for ten dollars at a nearby store.

Fate is smiling upon George Atzerodt. Nobody stops him as he leaves Washington. Soon he is in Maryland and, incredibly, it appears that he will escape the manhunt.

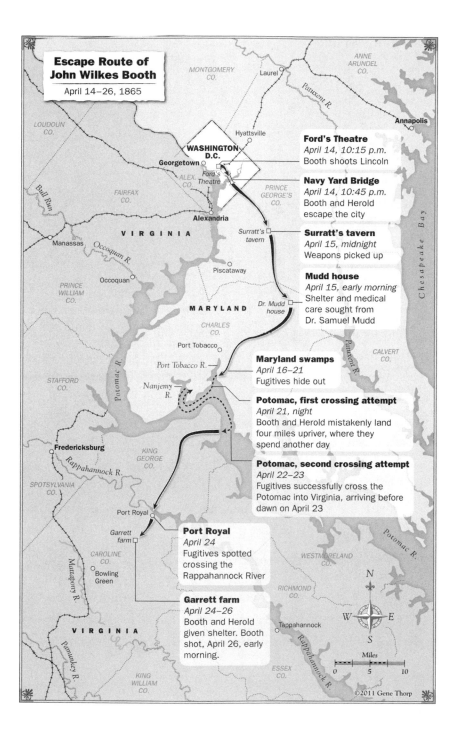

Escape Route of John Wilkes Booth
April 14–26, 1865

MONTGOMERY CO.

ANNE ARUNDEL CO.

Laurel

Patuxent R.

Annapolis

LOUDOUN CO.

Hyattsville

WASHINGTON D.C.

Georgetown

ALEX. CO.

Ford's Theatre

PRINCE GEORGE'S CO.

FAIRFAX CO.

Bull Run

Alexandria

VIRGINIA

Manassas

Occoquan R.

Piscataway

Surratt's tavern

Chesapeake Bay

Occoquan

PRINCE WILLIAM CO.

MARYLAND

Dr. Mudd house

CHARLES CO.

Port Tobacco

Potomac R.

Port Tobacco R.

CALVERT CO.

Patuxent R.

STAFFORD CO.

Nanjemy R.

Fredericksburg

KING GEORGE CO.

Rappahannock R.

SPOTSYLVANIA CO.

Port Royal

Garrett farm

CAROLINE CO.

Bowling Green

Mattapony R.

Port Royal

Potomac R.

WESTMORELAND CO.

RICHMOND CO.

Tappahannock

VIRGINIA

Pamunkey R.

KING WILLIAM CO.

ESSEX CO.

Rappahannock R.

N
W E
S

Miles
0   5   10

©2011 Gene Thorp

Ford's Theatre
April 14, 10:15 p.m.
Booth shoots Lincoln

Navy Yard Bridge
April 14, 10:45 p.m.
Booth and Herold escape the city

Surratt's tavern
April 15, midnight
Weapons picked up

Mudd house
April 15, early morning
Shelter and medical care sought from Dr. Samuel Mudd

Maryland swamps
April 16–21
Fugitives hide out

Potomac, first crossing attempt
April 21, night
Booth and Herold mistakenly land four miles upriver, where they spend another day

Potomac, second crossing attempt
April 22–23
Fugitives successfully cross the Potomac into Virginia, arriving before dawn on April 23

Port Royal
April 24
Fugitives spotted crossing the Rappahannock River

Garrett farm
April 24–26
Booth and Herold given shelter. Booth shot, April 26, early morning.

Chapter
41

SATURDAY, APRIL 15, 1865
Maryland Countryside
Noon

JOHN WILKES BOOTH IS MISERABLE. Flat on his back on a bed in the country home of Samuel Mudd, Booth screams in pain as the thirty-one-year-old doctor cuts off his boot and gently presses his fingers into the grossly swollen ankle.

After the assassination, Booth and David Herold rode hard all night, stopping only at a small tavern owned by Mary Surratt to pick up some rifles she'd hidden for them. Herold boasted that they'd killed the president. He also bought a bottle of whiskey so Booth could enjoy a nip or two to dull the pain. Then they rode ten more hard miles on tree-lined country roads. Every mile was more painful for Booth than the last.

Still, they're close. Very close. Mudd's estate is just north of Bryantown, Maryland, two-thirds of the way to the Potomac River.

Booth's pants and jacket are spattered with mud. His handsome face is unshaven and unhealthy looking. But more than anything else, John Wilkes Booth is helpless. He is completely dependent upon David Herold to lead their escape into the South. At a time when he needs all his intelligence and energy to complete the second half of the perfect assassination, he is in too much pain to think straight.

Dr. Mudd says he's going to splint the leg. Booth lies back and lets him, even though he knows he will no longer be able to slip his

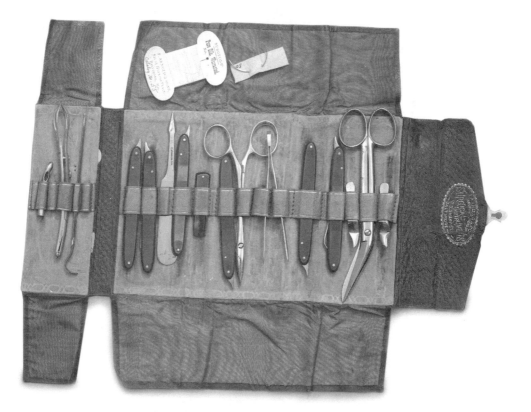

Dr. Samuel Mudd's medical kit.

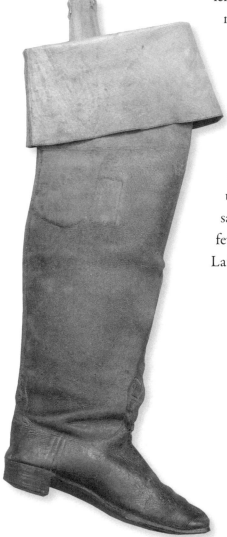

left foot into a stirrup. Now Booth must ride one-legged—if he can ride at all.

Mudd finishes splinting the leg, then leaves Booth alone in an upstairs room to rest.

Booth rolls over, closes his eyes, and falls into a deep sleep, sure that he is being hunted but unaware that more than a thousand men on horseback are within a few miles of his location—and that Lafayette Baker is now on the case.

John Wilkes Booth's boot that Dr. Samuel Mudd cut open.

Chapter
42

SATURDAY TO SUNDAY, APRIL 15 TO 16, 1865
New York City

L AFAYETTE BAKER IS IN HIS ROOM at New York's Astor
House Hotel when he hears that Lincoln has been shot. The
former spy is not surprised. His first thought, as always, is of finding a way to spin the tragedy for his own personal gain. Baker loves
money and glory. He understands in an instant that the man who
finds Lincoln's killer will have both wealth and fame. Baker wants
to be that man.

It's noon on Saturday when a telegram arrives from Stanton,
summoning him to "come here immediately and find the murderer
of our president."

Lafayette Baker takes the overnight train to Washington. Arriving at dawn, he travels immediately to the War Department, where
he meets with Stanton. "They have killed the president. You must
go to work. My whole dependence is upon you," the secretary tells
him.

Baker's first act is to post a reward for $30,000 leading to the

Lafayette Baker.

arrest and conviction of Lincoln's killers. He also has photographs of John Surratt, David Herold, and John Wilkes Booth plastered all around town.

Chapter 43

SATURDAY TO SUNDAY, APRIL 15 TO 16, 1865
Maryland Countryside

DAVID HEROLD NEEDS A BUGGY. With a buggy, he and Booth can travel quickly and in relative comfort. He asks Dr. Mudd to lend them his, but the doctor is reluctant; secretly harboring fugitives is one thing, but allowing the two most wanted men in America to ride through southern Maryland in his personal carriage would implicate Mudd and his wife in the conspiracy. If they were hanged—for that was surely the fate awaiting any Lincoln conspirator—their four young children would be orphans.

Instead, Mudd suggests that Herold join him and ride into the neighboring community of Bryantown to pick up supplies and check on the latest news. Herold agrees. But as they draw closer and closer to the small town, something tells Herold not to take the risk. A stranger will be too easily remembered by this tight-knit community. Herold lets Mudd go on without him and turns his horse back to the doctor's home.

It's a good thing he does. The United States Cavalry now has

Bryantown surrounded. They're not only questioning all its citizens—they're not letting anyone leave, either.

Having seen the Union troops in Bryantown before they saw him, Herold knows they cannot stay at Dr. Mudd's any longer. Just before dusk, he rouses Booth and helps him down the stairs and up into the saddle. Herold guides them south through the countryside, aiming for the Zekiah Swamp, with its quicksand bogs and dense forests. The few trails that exist there are almost impossible to see in the dark, and the pair are soon lost and frustrated. They turn back toward Mudd's farm but remain out of sight, plotting their next move.

As Easter Sunday dawns, Herold and Booth are camped in a grove of pine trees a quarter mile off the main road. A cold front is racing across Maryland, and they shiver in the damp swampy air. Booth isn't wearing a boot on his injured leg, and his foot and ankle are in

David Herold.

pain and quite cold from walking on swampy ground in the thin shoes he took from Mudd. Yet Herold doesn't dare make a fire.

After leaving Mudd's house, they find temporary refuge a few miles down the road at Rich Hills, the home of Samuel Cox, a former Confederate captain. It is not known exactly what was said between the men, but Cox does agree to help the assassins. Because Cox has forty former slaves living on his farm, it is too dangerous for Booth and Herold to stay on the property. Cox has his trusted foreman, Franklin Robey, take them to a thicket of pine trees where they can hide. Cox promises to send a man to ferry them across the Potomac River to safety. The rescue signal will be a soft whistle, a pause, and then another soft whistle.

So now they wait. Hour after brutally cold hour, they wonder who will rescue them.

Late Sunday afternoon, they hear the first whistle. Then a second. Confederate sympathizer Thomas Jones calls out to them in a low voice, announcing that he is walking into their camp.

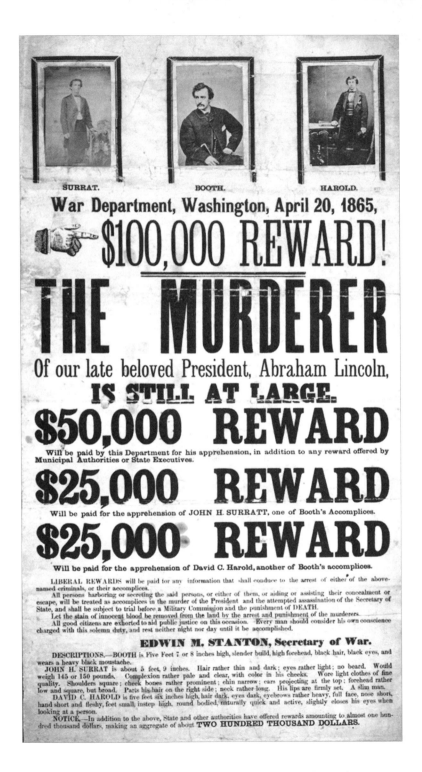

SURRAT.   BOOTH.   HAROLD.

War Department, Washington, April 20, 1865,

$100,000 REWARD!

THE MURDERER

Of our late beloved President, Abraham Lincoln,

IS STILL AT LARGE.

$50,000 REWARD

Will be paid by this Department for his apprehension, in addition to any reward offered by Municipal Authorities or State Executives.

$25,000 REWARD

Will be paid for the apprehension of JOHN H. SURRATT, one of Booth's Accomplices.

$25,000 REWARD

Will be paid for the apprehension of David C. Harold, another of Booth's accomplices.

LIBERAL REWARDS will be paid for any information that shall conduce to the arrest of either of the above-named criminals, or their accomplices.

All persons harboring or secreting the said persons, or either of them, or aiding or assisting their concealment or escape, will be treated as accomplices in the murder of the President and the attempted assassination of the Secretary of State, and shall be subject to trial before a Military Commission and the punishment of DEATH.

Let the stain of innocent blood be removed from the land by the arrest and punishment of the murderers.

All good citizens are exhorted to aid public justice on this occasion. Every man should consider his own conscience charged with this solemn duty, and rest neither night nor day until it be accomplished.

EDWIN M. STANTON, Secretary of War.

DESCRIPTIONS.—BOOTH is Five Feet 7 or 8 inches high, slender build, high forehead, black hair, black eyes, and wears a heavy black moustache.

JOHN H. SURRAT is about 5 feet, 9 inches. Hair rather thin and dark; eyes rather light; no beard. Would weigh 145 or 150 pounds. Complexion rather pale and clear, with color in his cheeks. Wore light clothes of fine quality. Shoulders square; cheek bones rather prominent; chin narrow; ears projecting at the top; forehead rather low and square, but broad. Parts his hair on the right side; neck rather long. His lips are firmly set. A slim man.

DAVID C. HAROLD is five feet six inches high, hair dark, eyes dark, eyebrows rather heavy, full face, nose short, hand short and fleshy, feet small, instep high, round bodied, naturally quick and active, slightly closes his eyes when looking at a person.

NOTICE.—In addition to the above, State and other authorities have offered rewards amounting to almost one hundred thousand dollars, making an aggregate of about TWO HUNDRED THOUSAND DOLLARS.

Chapter
44

MONDAY, APRIL 17, 1865
Maryland Swamps

Thomas Jones is a forty-four-year-old smuggler who has done time in prison, outlived his wife, and lost his home. He now earns his living by transporting anyone, including secret agents and diplomats, across the Potomac River. If any man can get Booth and Herold to safety, it's Jones.

On his first visit to the campsite, he merely wants to get a look at the men to see if they are capable of enduring what might be a very long wait until it is safe to cross.

His second visit comes one day later. Jones appears in their thicket, his pockets overflowing with ham, butter, bread, and a flask of coffee. In his hands, he holds the one thing Booth wants to see more than any other: newspapers.

Cavalry are combing the countryside, Jones cautions the killers, and he reminds them to be patient. It might take several days

The wanted poster for the Lincoln assassination conspirators.

before things die down. No matter how cold it gets, no matter how extreme the conditions, they must be prepared to hunker down in the woods until the coast is clear. As soon as it is, he'll let them know.

"I leave it all with you," Booth says unhappily.

Jones departs quickly.

With a sigh, Booth turns his attention to the newspapers. He reads about the extent of the search. But his melancholy soon turns to rage as he learns that his actions are not being applauded. Instead he is being labeled a scoundrel and a coward for shooting Lincoln in the back. Washington newspapers call him the war's ultimate villain and note that any "kindly feeling" toward the South or its sympathizers has disappeared, thanks to his actions. Booth's achievement is described in the Richmond papers as "the most deplorable calamity, which has ever befallen the people of the United States." And finally, the nation's most staunchly anti-Lincoln paper, the *National Intelligencer*, is now crying out that Lincoln was a true American hero. The very newspaper that the actor had once hoped would print the letter explaining his actions is instead portraying him as the most terrible man on earth.

Booth, overcome with despair, sets the papers aside. Then he takes out his diary. In it, he writes his reflections on killing Lincoln, just to make sure that his point of view is properly recorded for posterity. "I struck boldly and not as the papers say. I walked with a firm step through a thousand of his friends, was stopped, but pushed on," Booth writes. "I can never repent it, though we hated to kill. Our country owed all her troubles to him, and God simply made men the instrument of his punishment."

Booth writes and rants and writes some more. Then he sleeps. Then he awakens and writes some more. There's nothing else to do with his time.

John H. Surratt, Jr.

JOHN H. SURRATT.

IN HIS CANADA JACKET,

Entered according to Act of Congress by JOHN H. SURRATT, in the year 1868, in the Clerk's Office of the District Court of the District of Columbia.

Chapter
45

MONDAY, APRIL 17, 1865
Mary Surratt's Boardinghouse
Night

MARY SURRATT HAS BEEN A SUSPECT since the night Lincoln was shot. Detectives questioned her at two o'clock that morning, even as Lincoln lay dying. The widow was forthcoming about the fact that John Wilkes Booth had paid her a visit just twelve hours earlier and that her son John had last been in Washington two weeks earlier. When a thorough search of the house turned up nothing, the police left. No arrest was made.

Now they are back. One of her boarders, Louis Weichmann, has volunteered information to the authorities about the comings and goings of Booth and the conspirators at the boardinghouse.

It is well past midnight when police surround the house. She answers a knock at the door, thinking it is a friend. "Is this Mrs. Surratt's house?" asks a detective.

"Yes."

"Are you Mrs. Surratt?"

"I am the widow of John H. Surratt."

"And the mother of John H. Surratt, Jr.?"

"Yes."

"Madam, I have come to arrest you."

Three policemen step inside. Mary's twenty-two-year-old daughter, Anna, is also taken into custody. Just before they are led outside, Mary asks permission to kneel in prayer. She is a devout Catholic and prays "the blessing of God upon me, as I do in all my actions."

Major General Christopher C. Augur (seated, third from right) and his staff.
Augur was the commanding general in charge of all the troops responsible
for defending Washington, D.C.

The house is quiet. Her words echo through the half-lighted rooms.

Then there's another knock on the door.

When the detectives open it, they are shocked by the sight of a tall man with a pickax slung over his shoulder, wearing a shirtsleeve on his head like a stocking cap. His boots are coated with mud, and he is unshaven. As he steps inside, they see what appears  to be blood on his sleeves. The detectives quickly close the door behind him.

Lewis Powell, starving after three days of sleeping in the woods, instantly realizes he has made an error. "I guess I am mistaken," he quickly tells the detectives, turning to leave.

The police send Mary and Anna Surratt out the door, where carriages wait to take them to jail at the army headquarters of Major General Christopher Augur,

A photograph of Mary Surratt's boardinghouse, 1890.

the commander of troops in the Department of Washington. Then they focus their attention on the tall stranger with the pickax.

Powell gives his name as Lewis Payne and makes up an elaborate story, saying that he has come to Mary Surratt's at her request, to dig a ditch. The police press him, asking about Powell's address and place of employment. When he can't answer in a satisfactory manner, they arrest him. At the police station, he is strip-searched, and an unlikely collection of items, including cash, a compass, a pocket-knife, and a newspaper clipping of Lincoln's second inaugural address, are found in his pockets.

"Payne's" height and rugged build clearly match the description of Secretary Seward's attacker. The police summon William Bell, the young black servant who had given the description to the station.

When a lineup of potential suspects is paraded into the room before him, Bell marches right up to Powell. "He is the man," Bell proclaims. Powell's fate is sealed. He is sent to the same army jail holding the Surratt women.

Lewis Powell's pickax.

Chapter 46

TUESDAY, APRIL 18, 1865
Washington, D.C.

A sketch of a telegraph operator.

A T THE WAR DEPARTMENT, Lafayette Baker follows the progress of the soldiers' searches in Maryland. He also has his hired agents out searching, but his efforts to send and receive messages are hampered by the lack of telegraph lines through the Maryland and northern Virginia countryside. There is, however, a telegraph line at Point Lookout, a former Union prisoner-of-war camp at the mouth of the Potomac River. To keep himself informed of all activities in the area, he dispatches a telegraph operator to that location and orders him to tap into the existing line.

Now, safe in the knowledge that he has done everything that he can, Baker waits for that telegraph line to sing.

Chapter
47

TUESDAY, APRIL 18, 1865
Maryland Countryside
Afternoon

THE MOMENT DR. SAMUEL MUDD has been dreading comes while he is in the fields, working his crops. The Union cavalry unit galloping up the road is not there by accident. There are at least two dozen riders, including his cousin George. It was George to whom Mudd confided that two strangers had spent the night of Lincoln's assassination in his home. They spoke after Easter services, when Booth and Herold were still very much in the vicinity. Mudd took pains to state that his life was in danger should these two men ever come back. The story was a cover, intended to make it look as if he had no knowledge of the strangers' identities. It was Mudd's hope that George would act as a go-between, alerting the police to the fact that his Good Samaritan cousin might just have "accidentally" aided the men who killed Lincoln.

George, however, is a devoted Union sympathizer. Instead of the police, George has brought the cavalry. The riders dismount. Lieutenant Alexander Lovett is in charge and quickly begins to

A commemorative mourning pin honoring President Abraham Lincoln.

question the rattled Samuel Mudd to determine exactly who and what he saw.

Dr. Mudd, nervous and afraid, forgets the story he made up and rehearsed. Rather than present himself as eager for the "entire strangers" to be captured, he is vague and contrary. He mentions that one stranger had a broken leg and that he had done the neighborly thing by splinting it before sending the men on their way. When Lovett asks him to repeat parts of the story, he frequently contradicts himself.

Lieutenant Lovett is positive that Samuel Mudd is lying. But he does not arrest him—not now, at least. He is determined to find evidence that will link the man to the two strangers. He barks the order to mount up, and the cavalry trots back out to the main road.

Samuel Mudd, his heart pounding in relief, can only wonder when they will return.

Chapter
48

THURSDAY, APRIL 20, 1865
Maryland Countryside
4 A.M.

GEORGE ATZERODT HAS CHOSEN to escape by a northeast route, rather than push south like Booth and Herold. This takes him into a much more pro-Union territory. On the surface, Atzerodt's plan is an act of genius, allowing one of the most wanted men in America to hide in plain sight.

But the increasingly unbalanced Atzerodt is not a genius. His escape is not well planned. Instead he wanders from home to home among people he knows, accepting hospitality wherever he can find it. He dawdles when he should keep going. After four days on the run, he makes a critical mistake, boldly supporting Lincoln's assassination while eating dinner with strangers. His statements quickly make their way to police authorities.

Now, as Atzerodt takes refuge at a cousin's house in the small community of Germantown, Maryland, twenty miles northwest of Washington, a cavalry detachment knocks at the door.

There is no fight, no attempt to pretend he shouldn't be arrested. George Atzerodt goes meekly into custody and is soon fitted with wrist shackles, and a ball and chain on his ankle.

Two types of the wrist shackles used on the Lincoln assassination conspirators.

Chapter
49

FRIDAY, APRIL 21, 1865
Washington, D. C.
7 A.M.

O NE WEEK AFTER THE ASSASSINATION, the body of Abraham Lincoln is loaded aboard a special train for its return to Illinois for burial. General Ulysses S. Grant supervises the occasion. Also on the train is the casket of the Lincolns' third son, William Wallace "Willie" Lincoln, who had died in 1862 at age eleven of typhoid fever. Mary Lincoln has had Willie's casket removed from the cemetery, and now father and son will take the long train ride home to their final resting place in Oak Ridge Cemetery in Springfield, Illinois.

The president's funeral was held in Washington on Wednesday, April 19. Six hundred mourners were ushered into the East Room of the White House. Its walls and mirrors were covered with black cloth and the room was lit by candles. General Ulysses S. Grant sat alone nearest his dear friend, next to a cross of lilies. He wept.

Mary Lincoln is still so distraught that she will spend the next five weeks sobbing in her bedroom. She does not attend the funeral.

Abraham Lincoln's body lying in state in the East Room of the White House.

Immediately after the funeral, Lincoln's body was escorted by a military guard through the streets of Washington. One hundred thousand mourners lined the route to the Capitol, where the body was put on view for the public to pay their last respects.

And now, two days later, there is the matter of the train. The trip will re-create Lincoln's journey from Illinois to the White House four years earlier—though in the opposite direction. It will stop along the way in twelve cities and pass through 444 communities. In what will be called "the greatest funeral in the history of the United States," tens of thousands of people will take time from their busy lives to see this very special train before its great steel wheels finally slow to a halt in Lincoln's beloved Springfield, Illinois.

Abraham Lincoln's funeral procession on Pennsylvania Avenue.

*The steam engine Nashville that would pull the Lincoln
funeral train from Washington, D.C., to Springfield, Illinois.
Notice Lincoln's portrait mounted on the front of the engine.*

Chapter 50

FRIDAY, APRIL 21, 1865
Maryland Countryside
Noon

SAMUEL MUDD IS NOT HOME when Lieutenant Lovett and the cavalry return. Lovett sends farmhand Thomas Davis to find him. Mudd is having lunch nearby and quickly returns.

The terror of the previous encounter returns. Mudd knows that Lovett has spent the previous three days searching the area around his property for evidence. His nervousness increases as Lovett questions him again, probing Mudd's story for contradictions, half-truths, and outright lies.

This time Lovett does not ride away. Nor is he content to search the pastures and outer edges of the farm. No, this time Lovett gives the order to search inside the house to see where the supposed strangers slept.

Mudd frantically gestures to his wife, Sarah, who walks quickly to him. He whispers in her ear, and she races into the house. She returns holding two items: a razor and a boot. "I found these while dusting up three days ago," she says as she hands them to Lovett.

A typical house in the Port Tobacco, Maryland, area.

Mudd explains that one of the strangers used the razor to shave off his mustache. The boot had come from the stranger with the broken leg.

Lovett presses Mudd on this point, asking him if he knew the man's identity.

Mudd insists that he didn't.

Lovett cradles the long riding boot in his hands. It has been slit down one side by Mudd, in order to pull it from Booth's swollen leg to examine the break.

Lovett asks if this is, indeed, the boot the stranger wore.

Mudd agrees.

Lovett asks Mudd again if the doctor knew the stranger's identity. Mudd swears that he didn't.

Then Lovett shows Mudd the inside of the riding boot, which would have been clearly visible when Mudd was removing it from the stranger's leg. Marked inside the boot, plain for all to see, is the name J. Wilkes.

Dr. Samuel Mudd is put under arrest.

And while Lieutenant Lovett has just made a key breakthrough in the race to find John Wilkes Booth and David Herold, the truth is that nobody in authority knows where they are.

Lafayette Baker, however, has a pretty good idea.

Baker keeps a collection of coastal survey maps in his office. With what he calls "that quick detective intuition amounting almost to inspiration," he knows that Booth's escape options are limited. When news of the discovery of the abandoned riding boot makes its way back to Washington, Baker concludes that Booth cannot be traveling on horseback. He decides that Booth must hope to cross the Potomac River and guesses that the fugitive won't head toward Richmond if he does get across the Potomac, because that would lead him straight into Union lines.

Lafayette Baker is convinced that John Wilkes Booth's destination is the mountains of Kentucky. He will later write,

> Being aware that nearly every rod of ground in Lower Maryland must have been repeatedly passed over by the great number of persons engaged in the search, I finally decided, in my

own mind, that Booth and Herold had crossed over the river into Virginia. The only possible way left open to escape was to take a southwestern course, in order to reach the mountains of Tennessee or Kentucky, where such aid could be secured as would insure their ultimate escape from the country.

Baker studies his maps, searching for the precise spot where Booth would cross the Potomac. His eyes zoom in on Port Tobacco. In his memoirs he will quote a journalist as saying, "Five hundred people exist in Port Tobacco. Life there reminds me, in connection with the slimy river and the adjacent swamps, of the great reptile period of the world, when iguanodons and pterodactyls, and plesiosauri ate each other."

Lafayette Baker is wrong about Booth's effort to reach Port Tobacco—but not by much.

A photograph of Dr. Mudd's house in 1901.

Chapter 51

FRIDAY, APRIL 21, 1865
Maryland Swamps
Night

FIVE DAYS. FIVE LONG, COLD, MISERABLE DAYS. That's how long Booth and Herold have been in the swamp, scratching at wood ticks, shivering under thin, damp wool blankets, and eating the one meal a day provided by Thomas Jones.

The newspapers delivered by Jones continue to be a source of information and misery, as it becomes more and more clear that Booth's actions have condemned him.

Booth is just settling in for another night in the swamp when he hears the first whistle. Herold hears it, too, and is on his feet in an instant. Grabbing his rifle, Herold warily approaches the sound and returns with Jones. "The coast seems to be clear," Jones tells them, his voice betraying a sense of urgency. "Let us make the attempt."

Their camp is three miles from the river. Getting to the Potomac undetected means traveling down well-used public roads. Despite the darkness, they might run into a cavalry detail at any moment, but it is a chance they have to take.

Booth can't walk, so Jones lends him a horse. Herold and Jones help Booth into the saddle. The actor clings to the horse's mane with one hand to steady himself, the reins in the other, desperate not to fall off.

Jones tells them to wait, then walks ahead to make sure the coast is clear. Only when he whistles that all is well do they follow. Their pace seems frustratingly slow to Booth. But Jones is taking no chances.

When they approach Jones's house, Booth begs to be allowed inside for a moment of warmth. Jones won't hear of it, reminding them that his servants are home and could possibly give them away. Instead, Jones goes in and returns with hot food, telling the two fugitives that this might be the last meal they eat for a while.

They continue on to the river to a place called Dent's Meadow. Jones has hidden a twelve-foot-long boat at the water's edge, tied to a large oak tree. The bank is steep, and Booth must be carried down the slope. But soon he sits in the back of the boat, grasping an oar. Herold perches in the front. The moon has not yet risen, so the night is dark. A cold mist hovers on the surface of the wide and treacherous Potomac. Safety is just across the river in Virginia, where the citizens are pro-Confederacy. But getting there means navigating unseen currents that can force them far downriver—or even backward. The river is two miles wide at this point and patrolled by Union warships.

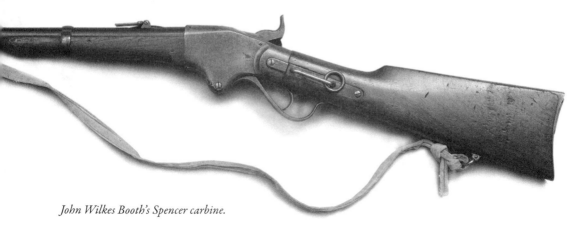

John Wilkes Booth's Spencer carbine.

"Keep to that," Jones instructs Booth, lighting a small candle to illuminate Booth's compass and pointing to the southwesterly heading. The actor has carried the compass since the assassination, for just such a moment as this. "It will bring you into Machodoc Creek. Mrs. Quesenberry lives near the mouth of this creek. If you tell her you come from me, I think she will take care of you."

"God bless you, my dear friend," says Booth. "Good-bye."

They shove off. Jones returns home, his work complete. His deeds will go unpunished. When his part in the conspiracy is revealed later on, the testimony will come from a black resident of southern Maryland and will be ignored.

Booth and Herold paddle hard for the opposite shore. That is, Herold paddles hard. Booth sits in the back and dangles his oar in the water under the pretense of steering.

Herold paddles for several hours against the current, but the combination of fast current and lack of light to help them see the compass to make sure they are heading in the right direction causes them to go the wrong way.

Finally, they land, four miles upriver from where they departed, still in Maryland. They are forced to hide themselves and their boat in the brush for yet another day.

And so, after one last, long twenty-four hours of hiding from the thousands of soldiers now combing the countryside looking for them, John Wilkes Booth and David Herold once again set out under cover of darkness, rowing hard for Virginia. This time they make it.

Next stop Kentucky and, eventually, Mexico.

John Wilkes Booth's compass.

*Newspapers in the North and the South
reported on the assassination for weeks after the event.*

MONDAY TO TUESDAY, APRIL 24 TO 25, 1865
Virginia-Maryland Border

SAMUEL H. BECKWITH is Baker's telegraph operator in Port Tobacco, Maryland. He telegraphs a coded message back to Washington, stating that investigators have questioned local smugglers and learned that Booth and Herold have gone across the Potomac River.

The information is not quite accurate. While it is true that Booth and Herold have crossed the Potomac, the information actually refers to a group of men smuggled into Virginia on Easter Sunday, not Booth and Herold. Lafayette Baker immediately reacts. A unit of twenty-six members of the Sixteenth New York Cavalry is sent by the steamship *John S. Ide* from Washington to Belle Plain, Virginia, about thirty miles south of Washington. With the Union cavalry are Baker's cousin, Lieutenant Luther Baker, as well as Colonel Everton Conger, a twenty-nine-year-old, highly regarded veteran of the Civil War.

The *Ide* arrives just after dark. The men immediately spur their horses down the main road of Belle Plain and then into the country-side, knocking on farmhouse doors and questioning the occu-pants. They stop any and all riders and carriages they encounter, pressing hard for clues.

But nobody has seen Booth or Herold—or, if they have, they're not talking. By morning, the cavalry squad is in Port Conway. Exhausted, their horses wrung out from the long night, the soldiers are starting to feel as if they have been sent to follow a false lead. Conger has promised them all an equal share of the more than $200,000 in reward money to be paid for the capture of Booth. This spurred them to ride all night, but now the prize seems out of reach.

Belle Plain, Virginia, in 1864 with Union troops
on their way to capture Richmond, Virginia.

This Union steamer is typical of the kind of ships,
like the John S. Ide, *that traveled up and down the rivers.*

Then, just as they are about to give up and go home, at a ferry crossing known as Port Royal, two men they question positively identify Booth and Herold. The fugitives had passed through the previous day with a small group of Confederate veterans. Whether or not they are still with the soldiers is not known.

By this time, the cavalry soldiers are exhausted, "so haggard and wasted with travel that [they] had to be kicked into intelligence before they could climb to their saddles," Lieutenant Baker will later recall.

But climb into their saddles they do, for hours and hours of more searching.

At two o'clock in the morning, at a handsome whitewashed farm three hundred yards off the main road, they finally come to a halt. The ground is soft clay, so their horses' hooves make no sound. The soldiers draw their short-barreled carbine rifles from the rifle boots attached to their saddles. Lieutenant Baker dismounts and opens the property's main gate. He has no certain knowledge of what they'll find. It is just a hunch.

Fanning out, the riders make a circle around the house and barn.

In a very few minutes, Lieutenant Baker's hunch will make history.

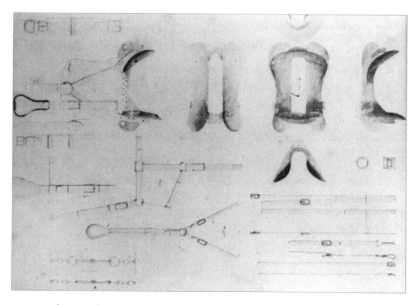

A drawing showing horse saddles and harnesses used during the Civil War.

Chapter 53

WEDNESDAY, APRIL 26, 1865
Garrett Farm, Virginia
Dusk

U NTIL JUST A FEW HOURS AGO, John Wilkes Booth was happier and more content than at any time since killing Lincoln. His broken leg notwithstanding, these three days in Virginia, with its pro-Confederate citizens and custom of hospitality, have made him think that escape is a possibility.

He's spent the last day at the farmhouse of Richard Garrett, whose son John just returned home from the war. The Garretts do not know Booth's true identity and believe his story about being a former soldier. He's enjoyed hot meals and the chance to wash and sleep. Then, an hour before sunset, came word that federal cavalry were crossing the ferry over the Rappahannock River from Port Conway to Port Royal.

Booth reacts to the news with visible fear. The Garretts, seeing this, grow suspicious and insist that both men leave. Booth and Herold refuse, though not in a belligerent way. Not knowing what to do and not wanting to create a problem with the two armed strangers, John Garrett sends them to sleep in the barn. Now Booth and Herold are hiding in a forty-eight-by-fifty-foot wooden structure filled with hay and corn. Worried that the fugitives plan to steal their horses and escape in the night, John and his brother William, armed with a pistol, sleep outside the barn.

Booth doesn't realize the Garrett brothers are outside guarding the barn, nor does he know that the cavalry is surrounding the place. All he is sure of is that at two A.M. dogs begin barking. Then a terrified John Garrett steps into the barn and orders the men to give up their weapons. The building is surrounded, he tells them.

"Get out of here or I will shoot you," cries Booth. "You have betrayed me."

Sergeant Boston Corbett.

Garrett flees, locking the barn door behind him. Then Herold says he wants to get out. He's sick of life on the run and wants to return home. He's done nothing wrong and wishes to proclaim his innocence.

"Captain," Booth calls out, not knowing the proper rank to use, "there is a man here who very much wants to surrender."

Then he turns to Herold in disgust. "Go away from me, damned coward."

Herold exits through the main door, wrists first. He is immediately arrested and taken away by the soldiers.

Lieutenant Baker calls to Booth, telling him that the barn will be set on fire unless he surrenders. "Well, Captain," Booth cries out, his old sense of the dramatic now fully returned, "you may prepare a stretcher for me. Draw up your men. Throw open the door. Let's have a fair fight."

Booth hears the crackle of burning straw and smells the sweet smoke of burning cedar. "One more stain on the old banner!" he yells, doing his best to sound fearless. No one quite knows what that statement means.

He looks across the barn and sees Lieutenant Baker opening the door. The actor lifts his rifle.

Booth hears the crack of a rifle and feels a jolt in his neck, and then nothing. Sergeant Boston Corbett, one of the men under Baker's command, has fired a bullet that slices through Booth's spinal cord and paralyzes him from the neck down. He collapses to the floor, the flames climbing higher and higher all around him.

Baker and Colonel Everton Conger pull Booth from the barn moments before it is engulfed in flames. The actor is still alive.

As with Lincoln, the decision is made not to transport Booth because any movement will surely kill him. But within two hours, he is dead. His limp body is thrown into the back of a garbage wagon.

The flight—and life—of John Wilkes Booth has come to an end. He is just twenty-six years old.

An illustration showing Union soldiers dragging the wounded body of John Wilkes Booth from the burning barn. This was on the cover of Frank Leslie's Illustrated News *on May 13, 1865.*

Chapter
54

FRIDAY, JULY 7, 1865
Washington, D. C.
Dawn

TWO AND A HALF MONTHS LATER, rounding up Lincoln's killers has become a national obsession. Secretary of War Stanton has personally taken charge of identifying the larger conspiracy that has grown out of Booth's single gunshot, pushing Lafayette Baker from the limelight. While some in the South call Booth a martyr and hang pictures of him in their homes as they would for any family member, Northerners are determined to see every last one of his fellow conspirators found—and killed. The jails are full of men and women who have been trapped in the spider's web of the Stanton investigation. Some have nothing to do with Lincoln's death, like James Pumphrey, the Confederate-sympathizing owner of a stable, who spent a month behind bars. No one is immune from suspicion. Federal agents scour lists of suspects, making sure no one is overlooked. One missing suspect is twenty-one-year-old John Surratt, whose mother, Mary, provided Booth and his conspirators with weapons and lodging.

Mary Surratt sits inside the old Arsenal Penitentiary in what will much later be the Army base named Fort Leslie J. McNair in south-central Washington, D.C., awaiting her fate. She's been locked up since her arrest on April 17. The trial of all the conspirators, including Mary, began on May 9, and 366 witnesses were called before it was over at the end of June.

After deliberating for three days, the nine-member jury finds Mary Surratt, Lewis Powell, George Atzerodt, and David Herold guilty. They will be hanged. As for Dr. Samuel Mudd, Michael O'Laughlen, Ned Spangler, and Samuel Arnold, their punishment will be the remote penitentiary of Fort Jefferson on the island chain of the Dry Tortugas, about eighty miles west of Key West, Florida.

No one is willing to speak up for the men who will hang. But Mary Surratt's priest comes to her defense. So does her daughter, Anna—though not her missing son, John. Mary Surratt's attorney frantically works to get an audience with President Andrew Johnson so that he might personally ask

Secretary of War
Edwin M. Stanton.

for mercy on her behalf. Her supporters say she was just a lone woman trying to make ends meet by providing weapons for Booth and his conspiracy and point out that she didn't pull the trigger and was nowhere near Ford's Theatre.

There is hope. Not much, but a little. The other three sentenced to hang are all part of Booth's inner circle. But Mary Surratt is not. Although President Johnson will not speak to him, Surratt's attorney continues to argue that her life should be spared.

The hooded conspirators taken from the Navy Yard to the site of their execution.

Mary Surratt spends the night of July 6 in prayer, asking God to spare her life.

In the morning, she refuses breakfast, and even at ten A.M., when her visitors are told to leave so that she can be prepared, Mary is still hopeful. Then she is marched out into a blazing summer sun. She looks up at the ten-foot-high gallows, newly built for the execution of the conspirators. She sees the freshly dug graves beneath the gallows—the spot where her body will rest.

Mary Surratt, Lewis Powell, George Atzerodt, and David Herold climb the gallows staircase. They are seated in chairs on the platform at the top. Their hands and arms are tied to their bodies— the men's with ropes, Mary's with white cloth. Their legs are tied together at the ankles and knees so that they won't kick wildly after the hangman springs the door. They are all then helped up. Each is placed in position over a gallows trapdoor. Next, white cotton hoods will be placed over their heads, then the noose of the hangman's rope.

"Mrs. Surratt is innocent!" Powell cries out, just before the white hood is lowered over his head.

Outside the prison, Mary's supporters gather. Time is short. But there is still hope. Soldiers stand on top of the penitentiary walls, just in case a rider approaches with a last-minute pardon. Inside the penitentiary, one hundred civilians have won the right to watch Lincoln's killers die.

"Please don't let me fall," Mary says to an executioner, getting dizzy as she looks down on the crowd from atop the tall, unstable gallows. He puts the white hood over her head. And, as he has done with the others, he then slides the noose over her head and draws it snug so the neck will snap quickly.

The death sentences are read in alphabetical order by General Winfield Scott Hancock.

Each trapdoor is held in place by a single post. At the bottom of the scaffold stand four hand-selected members of the armed forces. It is their job to kick away the posts on the signal from the hang-man. Suddenly, that signal is given.

The trapdoors swing open. The four conspirators drop six feet in an instant.

Stanton, who has witnessed the execution with other officials, lets the bodies dangle for twenty minutes before pronouncing that he is satisfied the condemned are dead. The corpses are buried in the prison yard.

◆◆✕◆◆

As the spectacle of the hangings fades from the public's preoccupa-tion, Lincoln's reputation grows. He becomes an icon, representing the fairness and strength of purpose that most citizens feel are America's best characteristics.

The Lincoln assassination conspirators just before they are executed.

Afterword

THE STORY OF LINCOLN'S ASSASSINATION continued long after his death. The primary conspirators met their fates within three months. Other key figures either profited or suffered from their roles. For many, Lincoln's assassination was the most important event of their lives. Here is a summary of their stories after April 14, 1865.

The body of **John Wilkes Booth** was returned to Washington from the Garrett Farm in Virginia on the *John S. Ide*. Booth's dentist and his personal physician were both brought in to testify that the body was Booth's. It was photographed and then the surgeon general, Dr. Joseph Barnes, who had tended to Lincoln in the president's final hours, performed an autopsy. The cause of death was determined to be a "gunshot wound in the neck," with the added

The front cover of Frank Leslie's Illustrated Newspaper *showing the mock burial of John Wilkes Booth's body in the Potomac River.*

notation that paralysis was immediate after Booth was shot, "and all the horrors of consciousness of suffering and death must have been present to the assassin during the two hours he lingered."

Dr. Barnes removed the third, fourth, and fifth cervical vertebrae from Booth's neck. These clearly showed the path of the bullet as it entered, then exited the body. The vertebrae are now kept at Walter Reed Army Medical Center, in the National Museum of Health and Medicine. Dr. Barnes then turned over his completed autopsy to Secretary of War Edwin Stanton, who also took control of the photographs made of the corpse and of Booth's diary, which was handed to him by Lafayette Baker.

The secretary of war wished the Booth situation to be handled with as little public outcry as possible, and this meant forbidding a public funeral. On Stanton's orders, Lafayette Baker staged a mock burial, wrapping the "body" in a horse blanket and publicly hurling it into the Potomac. However, this was just a trick to conceal the body's actual location. After the crowd onshore watched Baker dump a weighted object into the river, the ship traveled around a bend to the site of the old jail, on the grounds of the Washington Arsenal. The assassin was buried inside a gun box that served as his casket. In 1869, President Johnson ordered that the bodies of the conspirators be given to their families for reburial. Booth's remains were moved to his family's plot at Green Mount Cemetery in Baltimore.

Despite all evidence that Booth is actually dead and is buried in the grave bearing his name, various legends have maintained that he escaped into the South and lived a long life. In December 2010, descendants of John's older brother, Edwin, agreed to dig up his remain see if DNA from his body is a match for the DNA in the vertebrae housed at Walter Reed. As the chief historian for the Navy Medical Department noted, "If it compares favorably, then that's the end of the controversy. If it doesn't match, you change American history." As of this writing, the outcome of that investigation is still pending.

Mary Lincoln never recovered from Abraham Lincoln's assassination. She lingered in the White House for several weeks after the shooting, then returned home to Illinois, where she spent her time answering the many letters of condolence she received from around the world, and lobbying Congress for a pension. This was granted in 1870, for the sum of $3,000 per year.

In 1871, just when it appeared that Mary was recovering from her considerable grief, her eighteen-year-old son, Tad, died of a mysterious heart condition. This brought on a downward spiral of mental instability. Her only remaining son, Robert, had her committed to a mental institution in 1875. She spent a year there, during which she engaged in a letter-writing campaign to the *Chicago Tribune* newspaper that so embarrassed Robert, he had her released. Mary moved to the south of France for four years, living in exile in the town of Pau before returning to

Springfield. She died in 1882, at the age of sixty-three, and is buried next to her husband.

———◆◆◆◆◆———

Robert Todd Lincoln went on to a stellar career as an attorney and then public official. He served as secretary of war from 1881 to 1885, during the James Garfield and Chester Arthur administrations, and served as U.S. minister (as ambassadors were then called) to Great Britain from 1889 to 1893, under Benjamin Harrison.

A photograph of Robert Todd Lincoln at the dedication of the Lincoln Memorial on May 30, 1922. He was seventy-nine years old.

Although he was not present at Ford's Theatre when his father was assassinated, he was an eyewitness to Garfield's assassination in 1881 and was nearby when President William McKinley was assassinated, in 1901.

Robert Todd Lincoln died at his home in Vermont at the age of eighty-two, though not before attending the dedication of the Lincoln Memorial in Washington, D.C., in 1922. He is buried in Arlington National Cemetery.

Laura Keene would regret cradling Lincoln's head in her lap that night in Ford's Theatre. The assassination linked her troupe with the killing, and the attendant notoriety was hard on her already floundering career. The actress was eminently resourceful, however, and left America to tour through England before returning in 1869 to manage the Chestnut Street Theatre in Philadelphia. She later lectured on the fine arts and published a weekly art journal. Laura Keene died of tuberculosis on November 4, 1873, in Montclair, New Jersey. She was believed to be forty-seven, although she was often vague about her actual birthdate and may have been three years older.

Edwin Stanton did not live long after the death of Abraham Lincoln, and those years he did live were fraught with controversy.

Stanton clashed repeatedly with President Andrew Johnson over the process of reconstruction. Tensions between Stanton and Johnson got so bad that in 1868 the president fired Stanton. Stanton refused to leave the office. The Senate, which had openly clashed with Johnson over other key issues, began impeachment hearings, stating that Johnson did not have the authority to remove the secretary of war. Though Johnson escaped removal from office by one vote in the Senate, Stanton was the clear winner in the case. He retired soon after the vote, only to be nominated as a justice to the Supreme Court by the newly elected president, Ulysses S. Grant. Edwin Stanton died before he could be sworn in. The end came on Christmas Eve 1869; at the age of fifty-five, Stanton died from a sudden and very severe asthma attack.

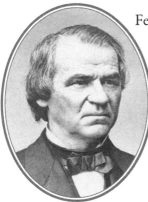

Few men could have successfully followed Abraham Lincoln as president, but **Andrew Johnson** proved particularly inept. His Reconstruction policies were bitterly divisive, to the point that he warred openly with Congress. He dodged impeachment but was not elected to office in 1868. Later in life, Johnson was reelected to the Senate, but soon afterward he died from a stroke, on July 31, 1875.

William Seward would live just seven more years after being attacked in his own bed on the night of Lincoln's assassination, but in that time he would undertake an activity that would leave an even longer-lasting legacy than the heinous attack. In 1867, while still serving as secretary of state and still bearing the disfiguring facial scars of the knife attack, he purchased Alaska for the United States. What soon became known as "Seward's Folly" would later be seen as a huge asset when silver and gold and oil were discovered in the new territory. Seward died on October 10, 1872. He was seventy-one.

Lafayette Baker became an instant celebrity for finding Lincoln's killer. The detective wrote a bestselling memoir in 1867, *History of the United States Secret Service*. In the book, he detailed his role in finding John Wilkes Booth. Several of his claims, including that he'd handed Booth's diary to Edwin Stanton, led to a congressional investigation into Stanton's role in the disappearance of the diary. Soldiers had given Baker the diary upon returning to Washington with Booth's body. Baker then gave it to Stanton, who locked it in a safe for almost two years, never telling investigators that he had the important historical document in his possession. The publication of Baker's memoir provoked a great public demand for Stanton to produce the diary. He did so reluctantly.

Baker became increasingly paranoid after the congressional investigation, certain that he would be murdered. And he was right!

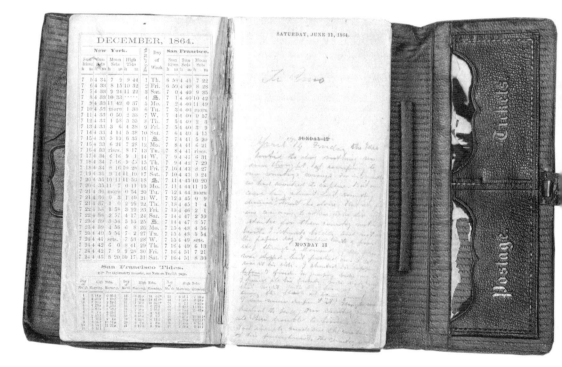

John Wilkes Booth's diary.

Just eighteen months after the investigation, he was found dead in his home in Philadelphia.

———◆•×◆×•◆———

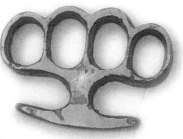

Abraham Lincoln's irresponsible bodyguard **John Parker** never presented himself for duty or tried to help in any way on the night of the assassination. Incredibly, Parker was not held accountable for shirking his duties. In fact, the first time he was seen after the assassination was when he showed up at a Washington police station the next morning. Formal

Brass knuckles carried by Lincoln's bodyguards. No photo of John Parker available.

police charges of dereliction of duty were brought against Parker, but once again he was acquitted. Three years later, after many attempts to remove him from the police department failed, Parker was finally removed for "gross neglect of duty." He went on to work as a carpenter and machinist. He died of pneumonia on June 28, 1890, at the age of sixty.

———◆•×◆×•◆———

Lincoln's responsible bodyguard **William Crook** had a more esteemed career, working in the White House for more than fifty years—a time that spanned the administrations of Abraham Lincoln to Woodrow Wilson. However, it was his relationship with Lincoln that he treasured most, and his 1910 memoir provides a vivid insight into the journey to Richmond and the events of April 14. William Crook died in 1915 from pneumonia, at the age of

William Crook at his desk in the White House in the 1890s.

seventy-seven. He was buried in Arlington National Cemetery, in a service attended by President Wilson.

After the war, **Robert E. Lee** applied for a pardon for his acts against the United States. Secretary of State William H. Seward did not file the pardon but instead gave it to a friend as a souvenir. The document wasn't discovered for more than one hundred years. President Gerald R. Ford officially reinstated Lee as a U.S. citizen in 1975.

After the war, Lee became president of Washington University in Lexington, Virginia. He died on Columbus Day 1870, at the age of sixty-three. Lee was not buried at his beloved Virginia home, Arlington, which had been confiscated during the war and redesignated as a U.S. military cemetery. Instead, he was buried at the university, which was renamed Washington and Lee University, in his honor.

Lee's counterpart on the Union side, **Ulysses S. Grant**, had an admirable career after the war ended. He remained in the army, helping to implement Reconstruction policies that guaranteed the black vote. He saw his popularity soar in the North. Elected president in 1868, he served two terms in office.

Grant's later years were filled with travel and, later, financial upheaval. After losing his entire fortune to bad investments in the early 1880s, he wrote his memoirs with the help of editor Mark Twain. Considered by many to be one of the best military autobiographies in history, Grant's life story was a bestseller. Royalties from the book guaranteed his family a comfortable life long after he died of throat cancer, on July 23, 1885. **Julia Grant** died on December 14, 1902, at the age of seventy-six, and lies alongside her husband in a tomb in New York City.

Major Henry Reed Rathbone, present in the box on the night Lincoln was shot, later married **Clara Harris**. In 1882, Rathbone was appointed as a U.S. diplomat to Germany. The following year, he went insane and killed his wife with a knife. He was institutionalized for the remainder of his life.

The fan Clara Harris carried the night President Lincoln was assassinated.

Boston Corbett, the man who shot John Wilkes Booth, received a handsome reward for the killing. He left the military soon afterward, first working as a hatter, then as assistant doorman for the Kansas state legislature. It appears that the mercury used in making hats, which was well known for causing insanity (giving rise to the expression "mad as a hatter"), caused him to become mentally unstable. In 1887, he was sent to an insane asylum after brandishing a revolver in the legislature. He escaped, then moved north to Minnesota, where he died in the Great Hinckley Fire of 1894. He was sixty-two years old.

Dr. Samuel Mudd, **Samuel Arnold**, and **Michael O'Laughlen** were all given life sentences for their roles in the assassination conspiracy. **Ned Spangler** (not shown) received a six-year sentence. All were sent to Fort Jefferson in the Dry Tortugas, a baking-hot group of islands about eighty miles west of the Florida Keys. Their jailers, black Union soldiers, had complete power over their daily movements. O'Laughlen died of fever while in prison, at the age of twenty-seven. Spangler, Mudd, and Arnold were pardoned by Andrew Johnson in 1869 and lived out their days as law-abiding citizens.

Thomas Jones, the man who helped John Wilkes Booth and David Herold escape into Virginia, was circumspect about his role in the assassination for many years. He was taken into custody shortly after Booth was killed and spent seven weeks in the Old Capitol Prison in

Washington, D.C., before being released. Even though he became a justice of the peace after the war, the tight-lipped former member of the Confederate Secret Service was ever after wary of persecution for aiding the conspirators. That changed in 1893, when he wrote a book telling his side of the events. Jones died on March 5, 1895, at the age of seventy-four.

Perhaps the most shadowy figure in the Lincoln conspiracy, **John Surratt** could have been instrumental in reducing Mary Surratt's sentence by showing that his mother's part in the assassination was that of passive support instead of active participation. But rather than give the testimony that might have spared her life, he fled to Canada after the assassination, where he followed the news of his mother's trial and execution. Surratt then went to England under an assumed name and later continued on to the Vatican, where he served in the Papal Zouaves, the pope's infantry unit. He was discovered and arrested but escaped. Another international search for Surratt soon found him in Alexandria, Egypt. Arrested again, he was brought back to the United States to appear before a judge. Amazingly, the jury deadlocked on his involvement. John Surratt was free to go. He died in 1916 at the age of seventy-two.

Mary Surratt was reburied in the Catholic cemetery at Mount Olivet in Washington, D.C. The petition to spare her life never got to President Andrew Johnson; his assistant, Preston King, kept the information away from Johnson. Apparently that action preyed on King's conscience. A few months later, King tied a bag of bullets around his neck and leapt from a ferryboat in New York Harbor; he was never seen again. He was fifty-nine years old.

Mary Surratt's grave.

A Walk Through Washington, D.C., in the 1860s

HOW A VISITOR FELT about a visit to Washington, D.C., in the 1860s depended entirely on the season. The best times were spring and fall. In May of 1864, the businessman George Templeton Strong wrote in his diary:

> *Loveliest weather. Spring manifested in ideal perfection. Genial warmth and bracing wind. . . . Trees budding and visibly developing from hour to hour. The air full of little cottony pellets thrown off from the American poplar, copious as the flakes of a January snowstorm.*

In summer, the city became unbearable. Everyone who could departed for the country. Abraham Lincoln and his family went to a cottage in northern Washington. On July 16, 1861, Strong wrote:

> *For of all the detestable places, Washington is the first in July. Crowd, heat, bad quarters, bad fare, bad smells, mosquitoes, and a plague of flies transcending everything within my experience. They blackened the tablecloths and absolutely flew into one's mouth at dinner.*

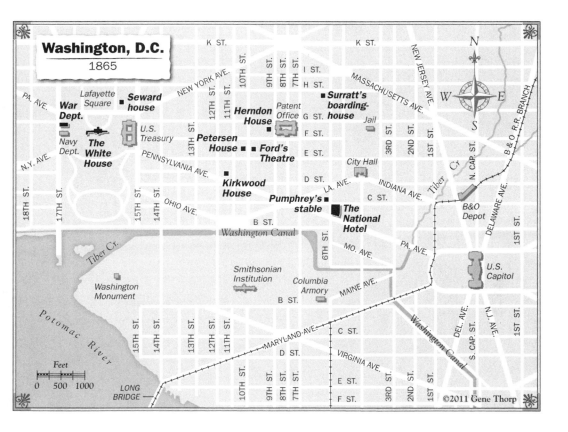

Washington, D.C.
1865

PA. AVE.

War Dept.

Lafayette Square

Seward house

Navy Dept.

The White House

U.S. Treasury

N.Y. AVE.

18TH ST.

17TH ST.

15TH ST.

14TH ST.

OHIO AVE.

PENNSYLVANIA AVE.

K ST.

NEW YORK AVE.

12TH ST.

11TH ST.

10TH ST.

9TH ST.

8TH ST.

7TH ST.

I ST.

H ST.

13TH ST.

Herndon House

Petersen House

Ford's Theatre

Kirkwood House

Pumphrey's stable

Patent Office

Surratt's boarding-house

Jail

G ST.

F ST.

E ST.

D ST.

Washington Canal

B ST.

Tiber Cr.

Washington Monument

Smithsonian Institution

Columbia Armory

B ST.

6TH ST.

LA. AVE.

City Hall

INDIANA AVE.

C ST.

MO. AVE.

MAINE AVE.

The National Hotel

Potomac River

Feet

0   500   1000

LONG BRIDGE —

15TH ST.

14TH ST.

13TH ST.

12TH ST.

11TH ST.

MARYLAND AVE.

10TH ST.

9TH ST.

8TH ST.

7TH ST.

C ST.

D ST.

VIRGINIA AVE.

E ST.

F ST.

3RD ST.

2ND ST.

1ST ST.

MASSACHUSETTS AVE.

NEW JERSEY AVE.

3RD ST.

2ND ST.

1ST ST.

Tiber Cr.

N. CAP. ST.

B&O Depot

DELAWARE AVE.

1ST ST.

B&O R.R. BRANCH

PA. AVE.

Washington Canal

U.S. Capitol

DEL. AVE.

S. CAP. ST.

N.J. AVE.

1ST ST.

N

W   E

S

©2011 Gene Thorp

Fall brought relief from the summer heat. But winter was on the way. And winter in Washington, D.C., could be awful. The roads were dirt and heavily traveled by horses and wagons. Winter meant cold rain and streets filled with thick mud.

Washington, D.C., was experiencing growing pains. The war brought thousands of people to the city. Some came to volunteer to fight. Others established factories and warehouses to make and store supplies for the Union army. Some of the Union troops were camped out in fields around the city, and tent hospitals were built there to treat the many returning war wounded. The population of Washington almost doubled between 1860 and 1870, going from 75,800 to 132,000.

Along the dusty or muddy streets you would see small two-story wooden homes next to six-story brick office buildings. At

A military hospital camp at Kendall Green, near Washington, D.C.

*A view of the Capitol building under construction
as seen from the mall in 1861.*

one end of what would become the National Mall, the Washington Monument was one-third built. At the other end, the Capitol was under construction, with scaffolding bracing the inside of its famous dome.

The White House looked much as it does now, but there were no fences around it. Washingtonians could walk through the lawns and gardens as they wished and even approach the president if they saw him.

Abraham Lincoln, Mary Todd Lincoln, and Their Children

AMONG THE GREATEST SORROWS in the married life of Abraham and Mary Todd Lincoln were the deaths of two of

A Currier & Ives lithograph of the Lincoln family.
From left to right: Mary Todd, Robert Todd, Thomas, and Abraham.

their children. They had four boys, and only one lived to be an adult. Doctors in the 1860s did not know as much about diseases and their cures as they do now. Although there is some debate about what Edward and William died of, we know that today they would probably have been cured.

———————✦◦✕◦✦———————

Robert Todd Lincoln was born on August 1, 1843, in Springfield, Illinois. His parents had been married about one year. Robert was named after his mother's father; his parents called him Bob. At the time, Abraham Lincoln was a lawyer and a novice politician. Robert went away to high school and college and then fought for the Union in the Civil War, although his mother didn't want him to.

Robert Lincoln served as secretary of war and minister to Great Britain and then worked as general counsel and president of the Pullman Company. He retired to Manches-

Robert Todd Lincoln.

ter, Vermont, where he pursued such hobbies as astronomy. His last public appearance was at the dedication of the Lincoln Memorial in 1922. He died in his sleep on July 26, 1926, at the age of eighty-two.

Edward Baker Lincoln was born on March 10, 1846, in Spring-field, Illinois. His parents called him Eddie. He died just before his fourth birthday. At the time, it was said that he died of consumption. Today we call the disease tuberculosis.

William Wallace Lincoln was born on December 21, 1850, in Springfield, Illinois. Willie moved with his parents to Washington, D.C., but died in the White House of typhoid fever on February 20, 1862. He was eleven years old. His younger brother, Thomas, also had the disease but survived.

William Wallace Lincoln.

Thomas Lincoln, known as Tad, was born on April 4, 1853, in Springfield, Illinois. He was very close to his older brother Willie and is said to have cried for a month when he died. Tad attended his father's funeral with his oldest brother, Robert. After leaving the White House, he and his mother moved to Chicago, traveled to Europe, and then returned home. Tad died of a heart condition on July 15, 1871. He was eighteen years old.

Abraham Lincoln, Mary Todd Lincoln, and Edward, William, and Thomas Lincoln are buried in the same tomb in Oak Ridge Cemetery in Springfield, Illinois. Robert Lincoln is buried at Arlington National Cemetery in Washington, D.C., an American military cemetery.

Abraham Lincoln and Tad Lincoln.

1858

1860

1861

1863

The Aging of Abraham Lincoln

The stress of the Civil War was hard on everyone. But no one carried a greater burden during the war than President Abraham Lincoln. This photographic sequence starts with a photograph of him in 1858, when he was forty-nine years old. The last photograph, taken in 1865, when he was fifty-six years old, shows how much the responsibility and anguish of the war aged him over the span of just seven years.

1865

1864

Twenty Important and Interesting Facts
About the Civil War

★ One of the reasons the Civil War continues to have an impact on the nation is that so many people died during the war. In 1860, the United States population was 31.4 million people. Originally, historians stated that roughly 620,000 soldiers and sailors, about 2 percent of the population, were killed in the Civil War. But in 2012, new research indicated that the death toll was higher, at least 750,000 men or almost 2.4 percent of the population. To put that number into perspective, if we took that new 2.4 percent figure and applied it to today's population of 313.3 million, the result would be about 7.5 million soldiers and sailors killed. No one knows how many civilians died in the war.

★ The Battle of Antietam on September 17, 1862, was the single bloodiest day in the Civil War. A total of 22,726 soldiers were killed, missing, or wounded.

A Currier & Ives lithograph of the Battle of Antietam.

★ The Battle of Gettysburg, from July 1 to 3, 1863, was the bloodiest battle in the war. A total of 51,116 soldiers were killed, missing, or wounded.

★ Though the song "Dixie" is considered the Confederacy's anthem, it was never officially adopted as such.

★ The South's nickname "Dixie" may have come from the boundary between Pennsylvania and Maryland, which was surveyed by Charles Mason and Jeremiah Dixon between 1763 and 1767 and called the Mason and Dixon Line. As Pennsylvania was a free state and Maryland was a slave state, it came to be regarded as the border between the free North and slaveholding South.

⚹ Several Civil War battles have two names. The reason for this is that the Confederacy usually named its battles after the town that served as the army general's headquarters. The Union armies usually chose the landmark nearest to their own lines, like a river or a stream. That is why, for instance, the Battle of Antietam, a name chosen by the North, is also called the Battle of Sharpsburg, a name chosen by the Confederacy.

⚹ Lieutenant General Winfield Scott was the top officer in the U.S. army at the start of the Civil War. Because he was seventy-five years old, he knew he was too old to lead men into battle. Scott thought that Robert E. Lee, in 1861 a colonel in the U.S. army, was the best soldier for the job. Scott offered Lee command of the new army being formed to fight the Confederates, which also meant Lee would be promoted to brigadier general. Though Lee had no love for secession or slavery, his home state was Virginia, which had recently seceded from the Union, and he could not lead troops against his home state. Lee regretfully refused Scott's offer, resigned from the U.S. army, and left for Virginia, where he became a general in the Confederate army.

⚹ Robert E. Lee was one of the many people who had family members who fought for the other side. One of his cousins, Samuel Phillips Lee, was a rear admiral in the Union navy.

⚹ Lee's father, General Henry "Light Horse Harry" Lee, was a hero of the American Revolution. His wife, Mary Custis Lee, was the great-granddaughter of Martha Washington, who was the wife of George Washington, America's top general in the American Revolution and our nation's first president.

* When Ulysses Grant was promoted to the rank of brigadier general, his father, Jesse Grant, thinking of all the many business failures his son had experienced over the years, told him, "Be careful. You're a general now; it's a good job, don't lose it."

* During the Civil War, the word *elephant* was one slang word meaning "combat." The phrase "seeing the elephant" meant going into battle.

The Battle of Gettysburg. This image is a stereoptic picture. When the card was slipped into a stereoscope the viewer had the illusion of seeing the image in 3-D.

✷ In 1862, Union troops were given small single-man tents to replace the large, heavy tents they had been using. Because they had to crawl into the tents like dogs, the troops called them "dog tents." That term later evolved into "pup tents."

✷ The Battle of Gettysburg had the largest concentration of Confederate artillery, 150 guns. The earsplitting roar of their cannon fire was heard as far away as Pittsburgh, 160 miles northwest.

✷ Many times during the Civil War, both sides would call a truce either at the end of the day or at the end of the battle so that the soldiers could gather their dead and wounded.

A Union drummer boy.

✷ Volunteers had to be at least eighteen years old to enlist. Some boys under the minimum age would write the number *18* on a piece of paper and insert it in their shoe. When a recruiter asked their age, the boys would say they were "over eighteen."

✷ Though boys under the age of eighteen were not allowed to fight, boys as young as twelve were allowed to enlist and serve in the noncombat position of drummer boy. Troop movement commands at the time were communicated by different drumbeats and bugle calls. Even though drummer boys couldn't fight, they had to be close enough to the battlefield that the men in their unit could hear their drumbeat orders. As a result, drummer boys saw as much combat as older soldiers, and a number of them wound up getting wounded or killed by enemy gunfire.

★ The youngest soldier believed to have been wounded in the Civil War was drummer boy William Black. He was twelve years old when an exploding shell shattered his left arm and shoulder.

★ Women were not allowed to enlist in the military during the Civil War. It has been estimated that as many as 400 women cut their hair short, disguised themselves as men, and fought as soldiers on both sides. Women were able to get away with this because recruiting inspections did not include a physical examination, and quite a few soldiers were too young to shave.

★ Dr. Mary Walker, who was the only woman authorized by the Union army to serve on the front lines with Union troops, became the first woman to receive the Medal of Honor in November 1865. So far she is the only woman to have received the nation's highest decoration for valor.

Frances Clayton, a female who as Jack Williams fought as a Union soldier in the war.

✷ The Civil War caused three amendments to be added to the Constitution, the second largest group after the ten amendments that
form the Bill of Rights. Known as the Civil War or Reconstruction
Amendments, they are the Thirteenth Amendment, passed in
1865, which abolished slavery; the Fourteenth Amendment, passed
in 1868, which recognized racial equality; and the Fifteenth Amendment, passed in 1870, which gave African-American men the right
to vote. Women would not get the right to vote until 1920, when
the Nineteenth Amendment was passed.

This unit of soldiers was charged with defending Washington, D.C.

Transportation During the Civil War

D URING THE 1800s, a person got from one place to another
one of four ways: by foot, animal (usually a horse), ship, or
boat. By the second half of the century there was a fifth option—
train. Obviously, travel by foot was the slowest, an average of two or
three miles an hour. Trains were fastest, but not by today's standards.
Though some trains were able to go sixty miles per hour, they were
exceptions, and such a speed was achieved only over a short distance. The average speed of trains was fifteen to twenty miles per
hour. By far the most common means
of transportation during the Civil War
was the horse.

In 1860, the North had approximately 4.4 million horses, and the
South had about 1.7 million. The average cost of these horses was about
$150 each, almost a year's pay for most

An inexpensive two-passenger buggy.

people. When the cost of caring for, feeding, and equipping the animals was added, it became more economical for people living in cities to rent horses from livery stables, much as people rent cars today. Daily rental prices varied, depending on the horse and planned use, but the cost was usually under a dollar a day. You could also rent vehicles to attach to your horse. Carriages came in a wide variety of models, styles, and price ranges for commercial and private use. They included stagecoaches, wagons, private coaches, broughams, cabriolets, phaetons, buggies, and surreys.

While the exact number of horses in Washington, D.C., during the Civil War is unknown, it's safe to say that the total reached the upper tens of thousands. An idea of what the city must have smelled like during its hot and humid summers is suggested by the goings-on at Giesboro Point Cavalry Depot, just south of Washington. From January 1864 to the end of the war, Giesboro managed a total of 170,622 cavalry horses and was estimated to have handled 700 tons of horse manure a day.

A cavalry depot. The long white buildings in the back are stables for thousands of horses.

Flags of the Civil War

THE UNITED STATES AND THE Confederate States of America had their own national flags during the Civil War. These banners were powerful symbols for each side, so much so that during the war soldiers willingly risked their lives to capture an enemy's flag or prevent their own flag from being taken. The United States had one flag design, the familiar Stars and Stripes, which changed only when additional stars were added to indicate that a new state had been accepted into the Union. The Confederacy had three official flags.

It's worth noting that even after the Southern states left to form the Confederacy, stars indicating their states were not removed from the Union flag. Since President Lincoln refused to officially recognize the Confederacy, the stars remained.

The United States flag got a second nickname during the Civil War, Old Glory. The phrase originated with William Driver, a retired shipmaster who lived in Nashville, Tennessee. He had named the flag as a young man, when he received it as a gift, and flew it on his ship during the 1820s and 1830s. When Tennessee

Old Glory showing thirty-four stars in its field.

seceded, Driver, a Union sympathizer, carefully stowed away the flag and waited. Union forces took control of the city on February 25, 1862, so he proudly pulled out his flag and, with an escort of soldiers, went to the tower of the state capitol and hoisted Old Glory. The nickname stuck.

The first Confederate flag, the Stars and Bars, was adopted on March 4, 1861. It had three horizontal bars of equal width (two red bars, and one white bar in the middle) and a blue field in the upper left corner containing a circle of seven stars to represent the seven original Confederate states. As other states seceded, the number of stars was increased to thirteen.

This design was thought too similar to the United States flag and on May 1, 1863, a second design, nicknamed the Stainless Banner, was authorized. This flag was white, with a red field in the upper left-hand corner containing a blue cross bordered in white and thirteen stars.

The Stars and Bars, the Confederate battle flag.

But this second design, with its large white section, was thought too similar to the traditional all-white flag of truce. A third national flag, nicknamed the Blood-Stained Banner, was authorized on March 4, 1865. It had a large vertical red stripe on its outer edge.

The Stars and Bars that people regard today as the national symbol of the Confederacy is actually a battle flag that was used by Confederate armies, not an official Confederate state flag.

Weapons of the Civil War

THE NEED FOR MODERN WEAPONS in large quantities inspired an industrial and invention revolution in both the North and South. Advances in mass production assembly enabled both sides to quickly arm their troops. But because most manufacturing plants were in the North, it was better able to supply its army throughout the war. The South suffered many shortages, and often its soldiers fought with weapons that had been taken from the bodies of Union soldiers.

Three of the many kinds of weapons used in the war are particularly important: the minié ball, the breech-loading repeating rifle, and the ironclad ship.

The minié ball, named after its inventor, Claude Minié, was a widely used lead bullet that had a tendency to shatter bones. At a time when medical knowledge and practice had changed little since medieval times, minié ball wounds were particularly life-threatening.

Most rifles and muskets at the start of the war were single-shot muzzle-loaders, that is, a bullet was inserted through the front, or muzzle, of the weapon. After shooting, the process was repeated. A good muzzle-loader could on average fire about three to four shots a minute. Breech-loading repeating rifles, which became available in the North in the winter of 1862, greatly increased a shooter's firepower. Instead of being inserted into the barrel from the front, bullets were loaded from its rear, called the breech, with the help of a spring-loaded hollow tube that held either seven (Spencer carbine) or fifteen (Henry rifle) bullets. As angry Confederates said, with some exaggeration, repeating rifles were "rifles you load on Sunday and fire all week."

A fifteen-inch gun near Washington, D.C., August 1865.

A photograph of Union private Walter Jones (left) and his New Testament Bible that stopped the minié ball bullets that would have killed him.

The most revolutionary weapon used in the Civil War was the ironclad warship, a ship covered entirely in iron. At the start of the war, all navies had ships with wooden hulls. The USS *Monitor* and the CSS *Virginia*, two ironclad ships, fought each other for two days in the Battle of Hampton Roads. The battle ended in a draw on March 9, 1862. From that point on, wooden-hulled naval ships were obsolete.

The ironclads Monitor *and* Virginia *fighting in the Battle of Hampton Roads.*

Medicine During the Civil War

MANY YEARS AFTER THE WAR, Dr. William A. Hammond, who from 1862 to 1864 served as the eleventh surgeon general of the U.S. army, said that "the Civil War was fought at the end of the medical Middle Ages." By that, he meant even the most knowledgeable doctors in the country were ignorant of the existence of germs and bacteria, the source of infections and diseases.

A Union army ambulance team practicing the gathering of wounded from a battlefield.

Of the hundreds of thousands of troops who died in the war, disease killed more than twice as many men as battlefield wounds. Before the war, hospitals didn't exist. Patients were treated at home. Even surgeries were performed at the patient's home. Such a system was impractical once the war began, and hospitals were quickly created. Most of the military hospitals were managed by a civilian organization called the Sanitary Commission.

For a soldier who was severely wounded in the hand, arm, foot, or leg, the most common medical treatment

An illustration of some farm buildings used as a Union field hospital. Note that on the left of the illustration, surgery is being performed out in the open under a cloth awning.

at the time was to cut the wounded flesh, or even the entire limb, from the rest of the body, a process called amputation. A typical surgeon's kit from the period contained a variety of knives and bone saws, thus inspiring the slang term for doctors "sawbones."

Amputation surgery was a brutal process conducted in assembly-line fashion. If anesthetic to render the patient unconscious, like chloroform or ether, was available, the patient was given that. Often, though, there were no painkilling drugs on hand. Instead, a bullet was placed in the soldier's mouth, and he bit on that when the pain became hard to bear. Union general Carl Schurz witnessed amputations being performed at a field hospital during the Battle of Gettysburg. He later wrote that after the doctor had done his examination, "the surgeon snatched his knife from between his teeth ... wiped it rapidly once or twice across his bloodstained

Four Union soldiers who survived the war. The soldier in the lower right was a prisoner of war who almost starved to death.

apron, and the cutting began." Good surgeons were ones who could work quickly, removing the limbs in a minute or less.

The survival rates depended on what was amputated. Patients who had a hand or fingers, or a foot or toes, cut off had the best chance of survival—the percentage of deaths being 2.9 percent and 5.7 percent, respectively. The deadliest amputation was at the hip. Sixty-six such amputations were done during the war. Fifty-five patients—83.3 percent—died.

As for President Lincoln, even today's medicine could not have saved him. His truly was a fatal wound.

Abraham Lincoln Time Line

Thomas Lincoln.

June 12, 1806 Thomas Lincoln and Nancy Hanks marry in Kentucky.

February 12, 1809 Abraham Lincoln is born in a log cabin on Nolin Creek in what is now LaRue County, Kentucky.

1817 Lincoln family moves to Perry County, Indiana.

October 5, 1818 Nancy Lincoln dies.

December 2, 1819 Thomas Lincoln marries the widow Sarah Bush Johnston.

March 1830 The Lincoln family resettles near Decatur, Illinois.

1831 Abraham Lincoln moves to New Salem, Illinois, where he works as a store clerk.

March 1832 Lincoln becomes a candidate for the Illinois General Assembly but will lose the election in August.

April 1832	Lincoln enlists in the Illinois militia for the Black Hawk War but does not see any combat.
August 4, 1834	Lincoln is elected to the Illinois General Assembly. He will serve four terms and begin to study law during this time.
1835	Lincoln becomes the local head of the Whig Party.
September 9, 1836	Lincoln receives his law license.
April 1837	Lincoln moves to the new state capital of Springfield, Illinois, and opens a legal practice to support himself when the legislature is not in session.
December 1839	Meets Mary Todd at a Christmas dance.
November 4, 1842	Abraham Lincoln and Mary Todd are married.
August 1, 1843	Robert Todd Lincoln is born.
March 10, 1846	Edward Baker Lincoln is born.
May 1, 1846	Lincoln is nominated as the Whig candidate for the U.S. House of Representatives.
August 3, 1846	Lincoln is elected to the House of Representatives, although the post doesn't begin until December 1847. He will serve one term.
1849	Lincoln leaves politics to become a full-time lawyer.
February 1, 1850	Edward Baker Lincoln dies of tuberculosis.

December 21, 1850   William Wallace "Willie" Lincoln is born.

January 17, 1851   Abraham Lincoln's father, Thomas, dies.

April 4, 1853   Thomas "Tad" Lincoln is born.

May 29, 1856   At the first Republican State Convention in Illinois, Lincoln gives a speech. He has helped to organize the new political party and will go on to campaign for the Republican presidential candidate, John C. Frémont.

June 16, 1858   Lincoln becomes the Republican candidate for the Senate, opposing Democrat Stephen A. Douglas. He delivers his "House Divided" speech on this day.

August 21 to October 15, 1858   Abraham Lincoln and Stephen Douglas participate in a series of seven debates throughout Illinois. The Lincoln–Douglas Debates, as they are known, focus on the divisive issue of slavery and establish Lincoln's national reputation.

1859   Stephen Douglas is reelected to the U.S. Senate.

May 18, 1860   Lincoln is nominated as the Republican candidate for president of the United States.

November 6, 1860   Lincoln is elected president.

December 20, 1860   South Carolina is the first state to secede from the Union. It is soon followed by Mississippi, Florida, Alabama, Georgia, Louisiana, and Texas, and they form the Confederate States of America. Eventually they will be joined by Virginia, Arkansas, Tennessee, and North Carolina.

February 11, 1861   The Lincoln family leaves Springfield, Illinois, for
Washington, D.C.

February 22 to 23,   Alerted about a possible assassination attempt in Baltimore
1861   (the Baltimore Plot), Lincoln disguises himself and secretly
travels by train through Baltimore to Washington, D.C.

March 4, 1861   Lincoln is inaugurated as the sixteenth president of the
United States.

April 12, 1861   In South Carolina, Confederate troops attack the Union
garrison of Fort Sumter in Charleston Harbor, beginning
the American Civil War.

The Confederate bombardment of Fort Sumter in April 1861.

February 17, 1862	Lincoln promotes Ulysses S. Grant to the rank of major general of volunteers.
February 20, 1862	Willie Lincoln dies of typhoid fever.
September 22, 1862	Lincoln uses the opportunity of the Union success at Antietam to issue his preliminary Emancipation Proclamation, freeing all slaves in the Confederacy.
November 19, 1863	Lincoln delivers his Gettysburg Address at the battlefield. It is regarded as one of the greatest presidential speeches ever delivered.
March 8, 1864	Lincoln and Grant meet for the first time at a White House reception celebrating Grant's promotion.
June 8, 1864	Lincoln is nominated for a second term as president.
November 8, 1864	Lincoln is elected to a second term.

The crowd at Lincoln's second inauguration, March 4, 1865.

March 4, 1865 Lincoln delivers his second inaugural address. John Wilkes Booth is in the audience.

April 4 to 7, 1865 Lincoln tours the captured Confederate capital of Richmond.

April 11, 1865 Lincoln, from a window at the White House, makes his last speech.

April 14, 1865 At Ford's Theatre, John Wilkes Booth shoots and mortally wounds Abraham Lincoln.

April 15, 1865 President Abraham Lincoln dies and Vice President Andrew Johnson is sworn in as the new president.

April 19, 1865 Lincoln's body lies in state in Washington, D.C.

April 21 to May 4, 1865 A funeral train, retracing Lincoln's first inaugural route through the nation, travels from Washington, D.C., to Springfield, Illinois. Lincoln, together with the body of his son Willie, is buried in Oak Ridge Cemetery.

President Lincoln's funeral car passing the Columbus, Ohio, state house during its trip from Washington, D.C., to Springfield, Illinois. At major cities, Lincoln's coffin was removed from the funeral train and placed in state so people could pay their respects.

Junius Brutus Booth in theatrical costume.

June 30, 1821	Renowned actor Junius Brutus Booth and his companion, Mary Ann Holmes, settle in Virginia, having left their native England.
May 10, 1838	John Wilkes Booth is born near Bel Air, Maryland.
November 30, 1852	Junius Brutus Booth dies.
August 14, 1855	Booth first appears onstage in Shakespeare's *Richard III*, starring two of his older brothers, at the Charles Street Theatre in Baltimore.
August 1857	Booth joins the company of the Arch Street Theatre in Philadelphia as an apprentice actor.
1858	Booth joins the Marshall Theatre company in Richmond.
December 2, 1859	As a member of the Militia Company F of Richmond Volunteers, which he'd joined the previous month, Booth

witnesses the execution of abolitionist John Brown. Shortly after this, Booth leaves the company.

December 20, 1860   South Carolina is the first state to secede from the Union.

March 4, 1861   Abraham Lincoln is inaugurated president.

April 12, 1861   Southern guns open fire on Fort Sumter in Charleston, South Carolina; the American Civil War begins.

November 9, 1863   President Lincoln goes to Ford's Theatre in Washington, D.C., to see *The Marble Heart*, starring John Wilkes Booth.

July 26, 1864   Booth meets with Confederate secret agents in Boston.

October 18 to 27, 1864   Booth meets with Confederate secret agents in Montreal, Canada. They give him $1,500.

March 4, 1865   Booth is in the audience as President Lincoln delivers his second inaugural address.

April 9, 1865   Confederate general Robert E. Lee surrenders to Union commander Ulysses S. Grant.

April 14, 1865   Booth shoots President Abraham Lincoln at Ford's Theatre.

April 26, 1865   John Wilkes Booth dies outside Richard Garrett's barn near Bowling Green, Virginia.

May 10, 1865   The trial of Booth's fellow conspirators begins.

June 28, 1869   John Wilkes Booth's body is buried in Green Mount Cemetery in Baltimore in an unmarked grave.

Finding Lincoln in the Nation's Capital Today

WHETHER YOU VISIT WASHINGTON, D.C., in person or online, the city has many memorials to Abraham Lincoln. You will be able to walk down streets he walked down and visit places he lived and frequented. Photographs, maps, and other information available online provide in-depth background about the city and the presidency.

THE WHITE HOUSE

www.whitehouse.gov and www.mrlincolnswhitehouse.org

1600 Pennsylvania Avenue

In the 1860s, there was not a fence around the White House. Residents of Washington and visitors could stroll through the grounds, and even enter the building. Military bands played concerts there regularly. The Lincoln family entertained on the lawn. Abraham Lincoln once said that he enjoyed the White House, except that people seemed to want him to make a speech whenever they saw him.

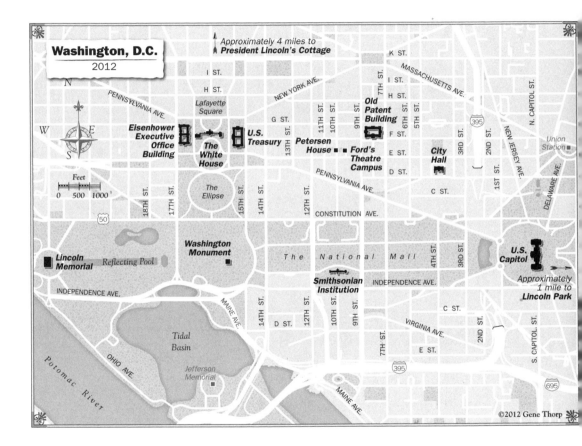

Washington, D.C.
2012

Approximately 4 miles to
President Lincoln's Cottage

N

W E

S

Feet

0 500 1000

50

PENNSYLVANIA AVE.

I ST.

H ST.

Lafayette
Square

**Eisenhower
Executive
Office
Building**

**The
White
House**

**U.S.
Treasury**

The
Ellipse

18TH ST.

17TH ST.

15TH ST.

14TH ST.

13TH ST.

12TH ST.

NEW YORK AVE.

G ST.

11TH ST.

10TH ST.

9TH ST.

**Old
Patent
Building**

**Petersen
House** ■ ■ **Ford's
Theatre
Campus**

F ST.

E ST.

D ST.

PENNSYLVANIA AVE.

K ST.

7TH ST.

I ST.

H ST.

6TH ST.

5TH ST.

MASSACHUSETTS AVE.

395

**City
Hall**

3RD ST.

2ND ST.

C ST.

1ST ST.

NEW JERSEY AVE.

N. CAPITOL ST.

Union
Station ■

DELAWARE AVE.

CONSTITUTION AVE.

**Washington
Monument**
■

■ **Lincoln
Memorial**

Reflecting Pool

The   National   Mall

4TH ST.

3RD ST.

**U.S.
Capitol**

INDEPENDENCE AVE.

**Smithsonian
Institution**

INDEPENDENCE AVE.

Approximately
1 mile to
Lincoln Park

MAINE AVE.

14TH ST.

D ST.

12TH ST.

10TH ST.

9TH ST.

7TH ST.

VIRGINIA AVE.

C ST.

E ST.

2ND ST.

S. CAPITOL ST.

OHIO AVE.

*Tidal
Basin*

*Jefferson
Memorial*
■

Potomac River

MAINE AVE.

395

695

President Lincoln's Cottage

www.lincolncottage.org
The Armed Forces Retirement Home
Rock Creek Church Road NW and Upshur Street NW
During the hot Washington, D.C., summers of 1862 to 1864, President Lincoln and his family moved to this cottage on a hill approximately four miles north of the White House. Here breezes tamed the humidity and the Lincolns could entertain friends and relax with their children.

Ford's Theatre Campus

www.fordstheatre.org
This museum complex, which includes several sites around Ford's Theatre, traces Abraham Lincoln's presidency, assassination, and legacy.

Ford's Theatre National Historic Site and Museum

511 Tenth Street
Audio tours and costumed interpreters highlight the history of Ford's Theatre and the path of Abraham Lincoln's presidency from his arrival in Washington to the moment he stepped into Ford's Theatre on April 14, 1865. Here you can see the flag-draped state box where Lincoln was shot, as well as artifacts such as John Wilkes Booth's derringer.

The exterior of Ford's Theatre as it exists today.

PETERSEN HOUSE

516 Tenth Street

Imagine the last hours of Lincoln's life and learn about the people who surrounded him during the vigil. You will see a reproduction of the bed in which the president died.

CENTER FOR EDUCATION AND LEADERSHIP

Tenth Street, next to the Petersen House

This new center explores the aftermath of the assassination, the hunt for John Wilkes Booth, and Lincoln's legacy.

LINCOLN MEMORIAL NATIONAL MEMORIAL

nps.gov/linc/

West Potomac Park, at the west end of the National Mall

This huge monument is one of the most important sites in Washington, D.C. It is almost a hundred feet tall and surrounded by thirty-six columns, one for each state that was in the Union at the time of Lincoln's death. In the central hall is the famous statue of Lincoln seated, with a thoughtful expression on his face. Carved on the walls to the north and south are the words of the Emancipation Proclamation and Lincoln's Second Inaugural Address.

The Lincoln Memorial in Washington, D.C.

EMANCIPATION GROUP STATUE

nps.gov/cahi/historyculture/cahi_lincoln.htm
Lincoln Park
East Capitol and Eleventh Street NE
This park is the first site in Washington, D.C., to be named for Abraham Lincoln. It is just east of the Capitol building. There are two statues in the park, of Mary McLeod Bethune, a pioneer educator as well as civil and women's rights activist, at one end and of Abraham Lincoln at the other. The statue of Lincoln is symbolic: he stands holding the Emancipation Proclamation before the figure of a kneeling black man. However, the statue does not acknowledge the active, influential roles played by many black Americans in the antislavery and civil rights movements. The model for the kneeling man was Archer Alexander, the last person captured under the Fugitive Slave Act.

EISENHOWER EXECUTIVE OFFICE BUILDING

Seventeenth Street NW and Pennsylvania Avenue
This new building is on the site of the old War Department Building where Secretary of War Stanton's office and the telegraph office once stood. It is just a short distance from the White House. It is not open for tours, but as you think about Lincoln walking here so many times at night to get news of the battles in progress, you will understand how different the president's life was in 1865.

Artillery. Weapons such as cannons or guns that work by launching large or small missiles of some kind (cannonballs, bullets).

Barrage. The repeated and powerful firing of artillery at a target.

Battalion. A grouping of soldiers in an army. During the Civil War, this was a military unit usually containing 400 to 800 troops, depending on the branch (infantry, cavalry, artillery, etc.), and commanded by a lieutenant colonel.

Bayonet. A swordlike blade attached to the front end of a rifle or musket, allowing it to be used as a stabbing weapon.

Bridle. Headgear used to control a horse.

In this staged photograph with a painted backdrop, the soldier at left has a bayonet attached to his musket.

An illustration showing Union cavalry capturing Confederate cannons.

Cavalry. Soldiers who fight on horseback.

Commissary. The organization that purchases and distributes food to the troops.

Corps. During the Civil War, a military unit usually containing between 10,000 and 15,000 troops, and commanded by a major general.

Detachment. Usually a small group of troops temporarily organized to carry out a specific purpose or duty away from the main unit.

Division. In the Civil War, a military unit usually containing about 6,000 troops and commanded by either a brigadier general or a major general.

Harassment. A series of repetitive, small attacks designed to delay or prevent an enemy's planned action.

Infantry. Soldiers who fight on foot.

Musket. A long-barreled firearm that has a smooth bore in its barrel, unlike a rifle's barrel, which contains grooves that cause the bullet to spin, thus increasing its accuracy.

Probe. Investigation by a soldier or a small group of soldiers of an enemy position in order to discover information about that enemy.

Reconnaissance. The gathering of information about an enemy.

Sentry. An armed guard in the military.

Shoulder board. A rectangular piece of cloth containing the symbol of an officer's rank.

Traces. The side straps, chains, or ropes used to attach a horse to a wagon.

Teamsters and their horse-drawn wagons.

Bibliography

Alexander, Edward Porter. *Military Memoirs of a Confederate: A Critical Narrative*. New York: De Capo Press, 1993.

Baker, Lafayette C. *History of the United States Secret Service*. Farmington Hills, MI: Gale, 2010.

Bishop, Jim. *The Day Lincoln Was Shot*. New York: Harper & Row, 1955.

Booth, John Wilkes. *"Right or Wrong, God Judge Me": The Writings of John Wilkes Booth*. Urbana: University of Illinois Press, 1997.

Corrick, James A. *The Civil War: Life Among the Soldiers and Cavalry*. San Diego: Lucent Books, 2000.

Crook, W. H. *Through Five Administrations: Reminiscences of Colonel William H. Crook, Body-Guard to President Lincoln*. Charleston, SC: Nabu Press, 2011.

Grant, Ulysses S. *The Personal Memoirs of Ulysses S. Grant*. Old Saybrook, CT: Konecky & Konecky, 1992.

Hatch, Frederick. *Protecting President Lincoln: The Security Effort, the Thwarted Plots, and the Disaster at Ford's Theatre*. Jefferson, NC: McFarland & Company, 2011.

Kaplan, Fred. *Lincoln: The Biography of a Writer.* New York: Harper, 2008.

Kauffman, Michael W. *American Brutus: John Wilkes Booth and the Lincoln Conspiracies.* New York: Random House, 2004.

Leale, Charles Augustus. *Lincoln's Last Hours.* Seattle, WA: CreateSpace/ Amazon, 2012.

Longstreet, James. *From Manassas to Appomattox: Memoirs of the Civil War in America.* New York: Mallard, 1991.

McPherson, James M., ed. *The Atlas of the Civil War.* Philadelphia: Running Press, 2005.

McPherson, James M. *Tried by War: Abraham Lincoln as Commander in Chief.* New York: Penguin, 2008.

Mudd, Nettie, ed. *The Life of Dr. Samuel A. Mudd.* New York: Neale Publishing Co., 1906. Also available online at archive.org/details/ cu31924032760930.

O'Reilly, Bill, and Martin Dugard. *Killing Lincoln: The Shocking Assassination That Changed America Forever.* New York: Henry Holt and Company, 2011.

Stiles, Robert. *Four Years Under Marse Robert.* Charleston, SC: Nabu Press, 2011.

Swanson, James L. *Manhunt: The 12-Day Chase for Lincoln's Killer.* New York: William Morrow, 2006.

Symonds, Craig L. *Lincoln and His Admirals.* New York: Oxford University Press, 2008.

Wagner, Margaret E., Gary W. Gallagher, and Paul Finkelman, eds. *The Library of Congress Civil War Desk Reference.* New York: Simon & Schuster, 2002.

Winik, Jay. *April 1865: The Month That Saved America.* New York: Harper Perennial, 2001.

Recommended Reading

Allen, Thomas B., and Roger MacBride Allen. *Mr. Lincoln's High-Tech War: How the North Used the Telegraph, Railroads, Surveillance Balloons, Ironclads, High-Powered Weapons, and More to Win the Civil War.* Washington, D.C.: National Geographic Children's Books, 2009.

Armstrong, Jennifer. *Photo by Brady: A Picture of the Civil War.* New York: Atheneum Books for Young Readers, 2005.

Denenberg, Barry. *Lincoln Shot: A President's Life Remembered.* New York: Feiwel and Friends, 2011.

Fleming, Candace. *The Lincolns: A Scrapbook Look at Abraham and Mary.* New York: Schwartz & Wade, 2008.

Freedman, Russell. *Lincoln: A Photobiography.* New York: Clarion Books, 1987.

Hansen, Joyce. *Between Two Fires: Black Soldiers in the Civil War.* New York: Franklin Watts, 1993.

Haskins, Jim. *Black, Blue & Gray: African Americans in the Civil War.* New York: Simon & Schuster Books for Young Readers, 1998.

Holzer, Harold. *Father Abraham: Lincoln and His Sons.* Honesdale, PA: Boyds Mills Press, 2011.

Judson, Clara Ingram. *Abraham Lincoln: Friend of the People.* New York: Sterling Point Books, 2007.

Kalman, Maira. *Looking at Lincoln*. New York: Nancy Paulsen Books, 2011.

McPherson, James M. *Fields of Fury: The American Civil War*. New York: Atheneum Books for Young Readers, 2002.

Meltzer, Milton. *Voices from the Civil War*. New York: HarperTrophy, 1992.

Robertson, James I., Jr. *Robert E. Lee: Virginian Soldier, American Citizen*. New York: Atheneum Books for Young Readers, 2005.

Smith, Lane. *Abe Lincoln's Dream*. New York: Roaring Brook Press, 2012.

Swanson, James L. *Chasing Lincoln's Killer*. New York: Scholastic, 2009.

Recommended Websites

There are many fine websites on the Internet about Abraham Lincoln and his achievements. Here are a few:

Abraham Lincoln Papers at the Library of Congress
memory.loc.gov/ammem/alhtml/malhome.html
The Library of Congress's collection of Abraham Lincoln papers includes approximately 20,000 documents, ranging from correspondence to drafts of speeches and important papers such as the Emancipation Proclamation.

Abraham Lincoln Presidential Library and Museum
www.alplm.org
The official site of the Abraham Lincoln Presidential Library and Museum is designed to promote the story of Abraham Lincoln in its entirety.

The Lincoln Institute
www.abrahamlincoln.org
The Lincoln Institute is an educational site designed to assist students and groups studying the life of Abraham Lincoln and the impact he had on the preservation of the Union, the emancipation of black slaves, and the

development of democratic principles that have found worldwide application. Links to specialized Lincoln Institute sites are available on the web page as well. These include "Abraham Lincoln and Freedom" and "Abraham Lincoln & Friends," among others.

Mr. Lincoln's White House

www.mrlincolnswhitehouse.org
A site devoted to the White House and living in Washington, D.C., during Lincoln's lifetime.

Abraham Lincoln's inkwell. Pens at the time were pointed wedges of metal attached to a handle. A writer dipped the pen point into a pool of ink contained in an inkwell, a process that had to be repeated until the writer was finished.

Recommended Viewing

American Experience: Abraham and Mary Lincoln: A House Divided. Director, David Grubin. DVD. PBS, 2001. 360 minutes, NR.

American Experience: The Assassination of Abraham Lincoln. Director, Barak Goodman. DVD. PBS, 2009. 82 minutes, NR.

The Civil War: A Film by Ken Burns. Director, Ken Burns. DVD. PBS, 1990. 680 minutes, NR.

The Day Lincoln Was Shot. Director, John Gray. DVD. TNT, 1998. 94 minutes, NR.

Gore Vidal's Lincoln. Director, Lamont Johnson. DVD. Platinum, 1994 (film released 1988). 188 minutes, PG-13.

The Hunt for John Wilkes Booth. Director, Tom Jennings. DVD. A&E Home Video, 2008. 94 minutes, NR.

Sandburg's Lincoln. Director, George Schaefer. DVD. Mill Creek Entertainment, 2011 (miniseries aired 1974). 298 minutes, PG-13.

Index

Page numbers in *italics* refer to maps and illustrations.

IT WAS
THE MOST NOTORIOUS CRIME
OF THE TWENTIETH CENTURY. . . .

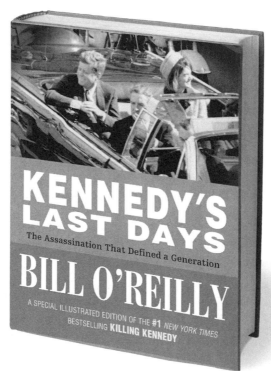

KENNEDY'S LAST DAYS

is history like you've never read before.
Turn the page for a sneak peek.

*Kennedy places his hand on an 1850 edition of the Bible brought
from Ireland by his ancestors.* [JFK Presidential Library and Museum]

CHAPTER ONE

JANUARY 20, 1961
Washington, D.C. 12:51 P.M.

THE MAN WITH FEWER THAN THREE YEARS to live places his left hand on the Bible.

Earl Warren, chief justice of the United States Supreme Court, stands before him reciting the Presidential Oath of Office. "You, John Fitzgerald Kennedy, do solemnly swear . . ."

"I, John Fitzgerald Kennedy, do solemnly swear," the new president repeats in his Boston accent.

John Kennedy was born into wealth and has a refined manner of speaking that would seem to distance him from many people. But he is an enthusiastic and easily likable man. He won the popular vote over Richard Nixon by a razor-thin margin, getting just 49 percent of the total votes. So not everyone loves JFK, but this is an exciting moment for the country.

". . . that you will faithfully execute the office of president of the United States . . ."

"...that I will faithfully execute the office of president of the United States...."

Eighty million Americans are watching the inauguration on television. Twenty thousand more are there in person. Eight inches of thick, wet snow have fallen on Washington, D.C., overnight. Spectators wrap their bodies in sleeping bags, blankets, thick sweaters, and winter coats—anything to stay warm.

The Marine Band stands in front of the Capitol during the inauguration ceremonies. [JFK Presidential Library and Museum]

But John Kennedy ignores the cold. He has even removed his overcoat. At age 43, JFK exudes fearlessness and vigor. His lack of coat, top hat, scarf, or gloves is intentional—this helps to confirm his athletic image. He is trim and just a shade over six feet tall, with greenish-gray eyes, a dazzling smile, and a deep tan, thanks to a recent vacation in Florida.

". . . and will to the best of your ability . . ."

". . . and will to the best of my ability . . ."

In the sea of dignitaries and friends all around him, there are three people vital to Kennedy. The first is his younger brother Bobby, soon to be appointed U.S. attorney general. The president values him for his honesty and knows that Bobby will always tell him the truth, no matter how brutal it may be.

Behind the president is the new vice president, Lyndon Baines Johnson, who is often called LBJ. It can be said, and Johnson himself believes, that Kennedy won the presidency because Johnson was on the ticket, which allowed them to win the most votes in Johnson's home state of Texas.

Finally, the new president glances toward his young wife, standing behind Justice Warren. Jackie's eyes sparkle. Despite her happy face today, Jackie Kennedy has already known tragedy during their seven years of marriage. She miscarried their first child, and the second was a stillborn baby girl. But she has also enjoyed the birth of two healthy children, Caroline and John Jr., and the stunning rise of her dashing young husband from a Massachusetts politician to president of the United States.

*John F. Kennedy takes the oath of office, administered
by Chief Justice Earl Warren.* [© Bettmann/Corbis]

"... preserve, protect, and defend the Constitution of the United States."

"... preserve, protect, and defend the Constitution of the United States."

Kennedy's predecessor, Dwight Eisenhower, stands near Jackie. Behind Kennedy stand Richard Nixon, Eisenhower's vice president and Kennedy's adversary in the presidential campaign, and Harry Truman, the Democratic president who held office before Eisenhower.

Normally, having just one of these dignitaries at an event means heightened security. Having all of them at the inaugural, sitting together, is a security nightmare.

The Secret Service is on high alert. Its job is to protect the president. The leader of the service, Chief U. E. Baughman, has been in charge since Truman was president. His agents scan the crowd, nervous about the proximity of the huge audience. One well-trained fanatic with a pistol could kill the new president, two former presidents, and a pair of vice presidents with five crisp shots.

". . . So help you, God."

". . . So help me, God."

The oath complete, Kennedy shakes Chief Justice Warren's hand, then those of Johnson and Nixon and finally Eisenhower.

Kennedy is the youngest president ever elected. Eisenhower is one of the oldest. The great divide in their ages also represents two very different generations of Americans—and two very different views of America. Those watching in person and those watching on TV agree: The future looks limitless and bright.

⸺

Now the 35th president of the United States turns toward the crowd. At the podium bearing the presidential seal, Kennedy looks down at his speech.

Kennedy is a Pulitzer Prize–winning historian, having received the award for his book *Profiles in Courage*. He knows the value of a great inaugural address. For months, he has worked over the words he is about to recite. That morning, he rose after just four hours of sleep and, pencil in hand, reviewed his speech again and again and again.

His words resonate like a psalm. "Let the word go forth from this time and place, to friend and foe alike, that the torch has been passed to a new generation of Americans—born in this

Kennedy's inaugural address is one of the shortest in history: thirteen minutes, fifty-nine seconds. [© Associated Press]

After the inauguration, the new president watches the parade pass. The press corps capture every moment. Seated next to Jackie Kennedy is the new president's father. Vice President Lyndon Johnson stands next to President Kennedy. [JFK Presidential Library and Museum]

century, tempered by war, disciplined by a hard and bitter peace, proud of our ancient heritage. . . ."

This is no ordinary inaugural address. This is a promise. America's best days are still to come, Kennedy is saying, but only if we all pitch in to do our part. "Ask not what your country can do for you," he commands, his voice rising to deliver the defining sentence, "ask what you can do for your country."

The address will be hailed as an instant classic. In fewer than 1,400 words, John Fitzgerald Kennedy defines his vision for the nation. He now sets the speech aside, knowing that the time has come to fulfill the great promise he has made to the American people. He must manage the issue with Cuba and its pro-Soviet leader, Fidel Castro. He must tackle problems in a faraway land known as Vietnam, where a small band of U.S. military advisers is struggling to bring stability to a region long rocked by war. And here at home, the civil rights movement requires immediate attention. Tempers in the South are flaring as more and more people demand equal treatment under the law for all races.

JFK surveys the adoring crowd, knowing that he has much work to do.

What he does not know is that he is on a collision course with evil—a course that will cut short the time he has to fulfill the promises he just made.

About 4,500 miles away, in the Soviet city of Minsk, an American who did not vote for John F. Kennedy is fed up. Lee Harvey Oswald, a former U.S. Marine Corps sharpshooter, has had enough of life in this communist nation.

Oswald is a defector. In 1959, at age 19, the slightly built, somewhat handsome drifter decided to leave the United States of America, convinced that his political beliefs would make him welcome in the Soviet Union. But things haven't gone according to plan. Oswald had hoped to attend Moscow University, even though he never graduated from high school. In-

Lee Harvey Oswald in a U.S. Marine uniform, in 1956. [© Corbis]

stead, the Soviet government shipped him to Minsk, where he has been working in an electronics factory. Oswald left the United States because he believes in workers' rights and thinks that workers in the United States are treated like slaves, but these endless days in the factory don't make him feel that he has any rights at all.

He was briefly important when his defection was reported by American newspapers. It was extremely unusual for a U.S. Marine to violate the *Semper Fi* (Always Faithful) oath and go over to the enemy. But now, here in Russia, he is anonymous, which he finds unacceptable. Lee Harvey Oswald needs to be noticed and appreciated.

Defection doesn't seem like such a good idea anymore, Oswald confides to his journal.

As America celebrates Kennedy's inauguration, he writes to the U.S. embassy in Moscow. His note is short and to the point: Lee Harvey Oswald wants to come home.

The 1959 photograph Oswald attached to his application for Soviet citizenship.
[© Associated Press]

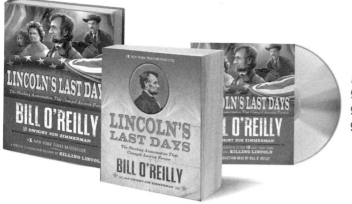

Lincoln's Last Days
978-0-8050-9675-0 HARDCOVER
978-1-250-04429-7 PAPERBACK
978-1-4272-2670-9 AUDIO

Don't miss more riveting reads from Bill O'Reilly!

Kennedy's Last Days
978-0-8050-9802-0 HARDCOVER
978-1-4272-3516-9 AUDIO

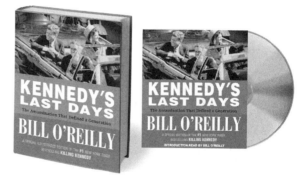

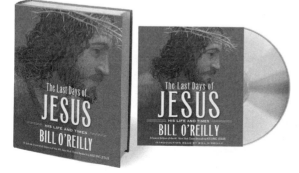

The Last Days of Jesus
978-0-8050-9877-8 HARDCOVER
978-1-4272-4111-5 AUDIO

SQUARE
FISH | mackids.com

Four score and seven years ago our fathers brought forth, upon this continent, a new nation, conceived in Liberty, and dedicated to the proposition that all men are created equal.

Now we are engaged in a great civil war, testing whether that nation, or any nation, so conceived and so dedicated, can long endure. We are met here on a great battle-field of that war. We have come to dedicate a portion of it as a final resting place for those who here gave their lives that that nation might live. It is altogether fitting and proper that we should do this.

But in a larger sense we can not dedicate— we can not consecrate— we can not hallow this ground. The brave men, living and dead, who struggled here, have consecrated it far above our poor power to add or detract. The world will little note,